Winning!

How Winners Think
What Champions Do

Edie Raether

ISBN 1-931219-02-8

Dedication

To my sons,
Charles Von Raether
and
Tory Jay Raether,
who have been my students and teachers,
my mentees and mentors,
and a springboard of support
both as children and adults.

They are my living "gold"
and
my forever one moment in time.

Acknowledgments

I sincerely thank
all of the many winners and champions
who have graciously shared
their experiences, insights, and wisdom
with me and with you,
for the heart and soul of this book
is from their generosity of spirit
to not just win
but to
make a difference.

Contents

ABOUT THE AUTHOR

Providing an ROI (Return on Intelligence), Edie Raether is an internationally recognized authority on the neuroscience of success and breakthrough thinking as a business strategy and the currency of the future. With expertise in emotional and intuitive intelligence, innovation, and influence, her revolutionary concepts – *MindShift, FutureThink, LeaderShift* and *TeamThink* – engage whole-brain thinking for personal renewal, strategic positioning, and organizational change. As a keynote speaker, Edie has empowered over 3,000 professional associations and Fortune 500 companies such as IBM, General Motors, JC Penney, S.C. Johnson, Oscar Mayer, the Marriott, ASTD, and MPI.

Edie is the author of *Why Cats Don't Bark, Sex for the Soul*, and *Forget Selling: 12 Principles of Influence and Persuasion*. In addition to numerous audio and video Change Mastery programs, Edie has also coauthored several inspirational and business anthologies.

Edie is an expert resource for hundreds of publications such as *The Wall Street Journal, USA Today, Prevention, Selling Power, INC Magazine* and *Reuters*. Edie has also shared the platform with such celebrities as Tom Brokaw, Patch Adams, Art Linkletter, and Bob Hope.

As a behavioral science expert, Edie has over thirty years of experience as a human asset manager and psychotherapist. She has also been a college professor and talk show host with ABC. Edie is the recipient of various Who's Who awards and the CSP (Certified Speaking Professional) award, which is the highest earned designation awarded by the National Speakers Association to fewer than eight percent of its membership.

Changing the Way the World Thinks... One Mind at a Time!

*For more information on Edie's speaking, coaching, and training programs, other books or her Change Mastery programs available on tape or CD, please visit her website at **www.raether.com** or contact her office:*

Performance PLUS
4717 Ridge Water Court
Holly Springs, NC 27540
919-557-7900 or 1-888-Raether

Email: edie@raether.com
www.raether.com

INTRODUCTION

As a psychotherapist and behavioral science expert for over thirty years, I personally felt challenged in my quest to discover the key characteristics in winners and champions from various fields. This book includes the findings from reports and hundreds of interviews with celebrities, change agents, Olympians, politicians, and successful CEOs as well as ordinary people doing extraordinary things. While each interview provided new insights, it also revealed common denominators that were consistent in all champions. As you take this "walk with the wise," may their experiences gently nudge you in the direction of your dreams and give you permission to begin your climb as you confidently whisper to yourself... "I can do that!"

My intention is not to provide you, the reader, with a superficial formula for success, but rather an awareness and understanding of the thinking patterns, attitudes, and most important of all, the responses of champions to disappointment, loss, and defeat. You will also learn their decision-making processes and problem-solving methods for personal empowerment, which will shed light on your path to success.

While winning and the success of being a champion is not necessarily happiness, happiness is always success and of course is based on one's personal preferences and values. Participation, personal commitment, and involvement are essential to the rewards of winning. In a recent study, it was revealed that people who won the lottery were not happier after their winning. In fact, it often added an element of chaos and disorder to their lives, rather than the anticipated freedom and elation. There obviously is little meaning to winning when one has not "earned" the victory or had the challenge or struggle of overcoming.

1

For example, what would it mean to hang a gold medal around your neck if you had never participated in the Olympics? The meaning of the medal comes only when it is a reflection of one's work, commitment, discipline, and efforts. The admission into sororities, fraternities, and even gangs involves initiation rituals which force people to endure a challenge, struggle or at their worst extreme, destructive activity. Terrorism is an example of misguided winning, one driven not by good but rather evil intentions.

Overcoming personal limitations and nature's boundaries have always provided a spiritual elation of transcending and rising above. We love the gamble and the challenge of testing our limits and beating the odds. Whether it is Evil Knievel flying over cavities in the Grand Canyon with his motorcycle; Dale Earnhardt, Jr. racing cars in the same sport that took his father's life; or Deena Kastor, after so many failed attempts, finally winning her first medal in Athens; all winners not only stretch their personal boundaries, but actually redefine human potential as being without borders, save for those that are self-imposed by a nervous mind. Athens was also the triumphant territory for male runner Hicham El Guerrouj of Morocco. Hicham took home the gold after several heroic attempts in previous Olympiads: a close call in Sydney and a sad stumble in Atlanta. His last 800 meters in the 1,500 meter race broke all records as he came from behind to claim his much deserved medal. Even the runners he had just defeated hugged him and shared his joy which was so contagious that everyone watching, even those of us thousands of miles away, were part of his magical moment.

Competition is not without compassion, as demonstrated by Michael Phelps who came home with eight medals, six being gold. Michael chose to relinquish his secure position on the US relay swim team to offer the experience of winning to another teammate. If you are still not convinced that winning is mostly mental, reflect on the spirit of women runners such as Catherine Ndereba of Kenya and Mizuki Noguchi of Japan, a 4'11" runner who experienced an adrenalin rush and pulled ahead of the lengthy legs of her competition to claim the gold.

As in David and Goliath, we all rejoice in the victories of the little guy. The winning presence of smaller countries such as Israel and Greece; struggling countries such as Iraq; and emerging countries such as the Czech Republic; renews the undying faith of the human spirit in all of us.

Oftentimes, winning is not just a personal victory but a collective experience and political/social statement as well. Billie Jean King, renown tennis champion, recalls the pressure and weight she felt on the courts, knowing her victory would alter the position of women in the world of sports, and it has. In the 2004 Olympics, forty-eight percent of the participants from the USA were women, and forty percent from other participating countries were women. I'm not sure how the Greeks of 2,800 years ago would have handled that one! Pioneers and change agents, however, do pay a price. Billie Jean King admitted that after all these years, she still feels somewhat fatigued and stressed out from that one moment in time.

As the five-time NFL champion Green Bay Packer coach Vince Lombardi said, "Winning isn't everything – but wanting to win is." That philosophy was most dramatically exhibited by Gabriele Andersen, another female marathon runner, who was so frightfully delirious that she literally staggered across the finish line. In that life-threatening marathon run, winning seemed to be more important than survival, or, in a sense, may actually have been her survival.

Sometimes our losses are our greatest victories and our bronze is symbolic gold. For example, a Brazilian male marathon runner was attacked and pushed out of the race by a madman who leaped from the crowd. For most the race would have been over, but rather than accept the unfair fate, he jumped back up, got back in the race and took third.

Although life is not fair, we always have a choice. We can pout and become angry, hardened, bitter, and defeated, or we can get back into the race and win. In fact, one of the things I learned in my interviews with so many magical people was that winning was less about the prize and more about the process. It was more about how one dealt with losing and losses. In my interview with Bonnie St John, an amputee skier and medalist in the 1984 Paralympics in Austria, she confirmed that the one thing Olympians most share in common is loss. "Olympians lose more than anyone else. If you're not willing to be bad at something, you'll never be good at it. The champion mindset is a willingness to lose, otherwise who would try." Bonnie also introduced me to another aspect of winning. "It is not how fast you ski, but how fast you get back up." Bonnie related that although she skied faster than the German gold medalist, she did not get back up as quickly after both had fallen. That one insight could inspire you to bring home your gold. It certainly did for Paul Hamm, the USA gymnast who, after a most disappointing performance, came back to grab the gold. Certainly Babe Ruth's record is testimony to the fact that it was not how many times he struck out, but how often he hit a home run.   Just for the record, although Babe Ruth had 714 home runs, he also struck out 1,330 times.

You will also discover from Frank Maguire, one of the pioneering fathers of Federal Express, how a sense of purpose fuels passion, and how having a purpose propelled Nick Irons, author of *Swim Lessons*, to swim the Mississippi River—almost 1,600 miles of wavy waters—followed by a quick bike ride of 10,000 miles around the entire U.S. Erik Weihenmayer, author of *Touch the Top of the World*, is the blind mountain climber who summited Mt. Everest. Erik is a breath-taking example of the courage and never-say-die attitude of champions. In his interview with Liz Brunner, Erik summed up the spirit and driving force of winners. "It's like you know you're doing something that human beings shouldn't be doing, you know? I like the spiritual feeling of being on a mountain…Why climb when I can't see the view from the top? You don't climb for the view. No one suffers the way you do on a mountain for a beautiful view. The real beauty of life happens on the side of the mountain, not the top." Weihenmayer admits he feels most alive sitting on the side of a mountain. (Note: not the sidelines.)

There are those who are champions of survival, such as Aron Ralston, another mountain climber. On that miraculous day in March of 2004, he was able to sever his arm out from under an 800-pound bolder to save his life when he literally got caught *Between a Rock and a Hard Place*, the title of his book.

Whether champions are made or born, winning, like happiness and success, is one of the most coveted emotional states we all wish to experience. Many seek the nirvana of winning by spending their extra chump change or even their life's savings on the state lottery or local casino. Others choose a more challenging route such as the discipline required to be chosen the valedictorian, or collect a mantel full of trophies and "letters" as the high school sports hero. Winners may also claim the honors of being the captain of the cheerleader squad or armor themselves with bronze, silver, and gold medals earned at the state's music tournament. Certainly Olympians require a thirst for the rewards of victory and are willing to pay the price and sacrifice of many hours of disciplined practice and rehearsals. Since many of the rewards provide no monetary gain, and quite often participation is an expense to the participant, there is obviously an intangible reward that lures thousands into the arena of potential winnings. In fact, for many political and social change agents such as Mother Teresa, Mahatma Gandhi, and Rosa Parks, it was simply a commitment to do what was right, what needed to be done, and to make a difference.

In this world of push-button love and instant success, this book reveals the seduction of winning that motivates millions to make the sacrifice and pay the price. Pleasure certainly offers its own rewards, and like all addictions, the pleasurable feeling state of winning offers its own intoxication. Those who have never experienced the natural highs of winning are not hooked on the adrenalin rush and thus are not motivated to pay the price of the glory that could be theirs. When we experience the joys of winning earlier in life, the emotional impact and desire for more of the champion experience is that much greater.

Whether it is winning a relay race at the city park, twirling the baton, or turning somersaults and hearing the obligatory applause of family fans, we gain a sense of power, control, and mastery. This creates a spiritual elation resulting from beating the odds and overcoming self-imposed human limitations. The many inspiring stories of the masters will enlighten and empower you not only to summit the mountains in your life, but more importantly to experience the joy and beauty of life that happens in climbing.

L'Chaim - To Life!

6   Winning!

CHAPTER ONE

MINDSHIFT:
CHANGE YOUR MIND – CHANGE YOUR LIFE

> *"The longer I live, the more I am certain that the great*
> *difference between the great and insignificant is energy –*
> *invincible determination."*
> **Sir Thomas Fowell Buxton**

Thoughts become things and you become your thoughts. Your outer world is very much a reflection of your inner world. You become what you think, since your thoughts fuel and provide energy to the physical manifestations of the realities you create. If you think about success and confidence, you will feel strong and empowered and perform with competence. If you are focused on the "what ifs" and anticipate failure, your performance will reflect the negative thoughts you programmed into your mind. Your thoughts are the seeds of the realities you create. Thoughts trigger your emotional state which determines your behavior and level of performance. Your life is a web of interconnections between thoughts, feelings, and actions woven together by personal choices.

Just as your hopes and aspirations are triggers to the results you experience, so too are your hopes and aspirations. The choices we make seem to be contingent upon more than just desire and willpower, but also how our hardware is wired which affects how we perceive reality. Without getting into the intricate factors of the neuropsychology of success, the relay switch in our brain called the RAS (reticular activating system) weighs out the value of each situation in terms of personal meaning and relevance and then sends it to long term memory storage or simply deletes it. The more emotional impact there is in any given

7

event or situation, the deeper the imprint on the mind. The crucial factor in determining our thoughts and attitudes is our perception, which is a complex internal reaction to an outside event. We are far more selective in what we perceive and choose to be aware of than you can even imagine. "Concept louses up percept." In other words, we perceive and selectively seek out that which our minds anticipate and expect which explains the roots of prejudice. Once we have a specific conception or visual expectation it creates a blueprint in our mind that triggers the RAS to work unconsciously 24/7 at transforming thoughts into actions and dreams into realities.

What the Mind Sees the Body Believes

In my interview with Elaine McPherson, a very successful entrepreneur and businesswoman in Asheville, North Carolina, it was clearly confirmed that a visual image of our desired dreams and successes, especially at a younger age, will eventually become a physical reality. Elaine reports that as a young mountain girl, her parents divorced when she was 5, she quit school and married at the age of 15, and gave birth to her first child at 16.

Elaine recalls that while listening to the Grand Ole Opry on the radio at age 10, she would see herself dancing on that most famous stage. It was only ten years later, at the age of 20, that Elaine not only danced with the Grand Ole Opry but also clogged her happy heels at Carnegie Hall in New York City. The winning spirit tends to be addictive and thus she transferred that same breakthrough thinking and winning spirit to breaking barriers in the business world. Although her childhood environment did not lend the ideal support of dance lessons at age 5 and a "soccer mom" who might coach and support her daughter to think big, there were two crucial factors to Elaine's success. One was she was born with an overdose of chutzpah, and the other was she had a vision, a mental blueprint and visual conception of who she might become and what she might accomplish. What the mind sees, the body believes. Once the pictures in your mind are crystallized, you cannot *not* make it happen. I am sure if you tickle your brain a bit you will think of barriers you may have broken as well, or friends who may have beaten the odds with less than an ideal environment or support system. Another example is Hilary Swank , best actress in *Million Dollar Baby*. As she received her second Oscar Hilary said, "I don't know what I did in this life to deserve all this. I'm just a girl from a trailer park who had a dream."

Internal Knowing

Let me share just a few more examples of some of my friends and colleagues in the National Speakers Association. Desi Williamson, author of *Get Off Your Assets*, explained, "We all come into this world naked." While Desi agrees with my previous writings on all of us coming into this world with a soul's code, he also sees it not as a formula or a destiny as much as that with which we need to be in alignment. Desi also emphasized that the real winners are those people who make a difference, overcome adversity, and then follow through with their plans. With the endorsement of all interviewed champions, Desi emphasized the importance of having some adversity and struggle in one's life and that too much success too early or too fast, without opposition, can be a detriment. Certainly we have all witnessed that with the suicide rate, drug abuse, and insanities exhibited by overnight rock stars and actors, actresses, and other celebrities. It simply does not work.

Desi also emphasized the power of belief or "internal knowing" being more important than hope, which often has an element of doubt. Desi had to overcome a few adversities himself. His mother was but 15 years old and his dad 19 when he was born. Due to an environment of physical abuse, at the early age of 11 young Desi took control of his life and his destiny by packing his clothes in the only luggage available – a paper bag – and had saved his pennies for a cab drive across town to the loving, open arms of a supportive grandmother. The question is what was it in Desi's DNA that propelled him to make a constructive decision and take positive action when a younger brother who did not accept that same personal responsibility ended up in prison for twenty years. There are obviously points of decision in all of our lives that become dramatic turning points.

While dining at Nola's in New Orleans, we were served by Janette, a young waitress with a glow that engaged all of us. After analyzing her smile, her energy, and her powerful presence, I finally inquired on what her source of strength might be. She confessed she had lost her mother at a young age as well as her father who was never really alive in her life, and added that her brothers were in prison. Her only explanation was, "It just comes from inside me." Are you tapping into what is inside you?

Words Create Blueprints of Success

Nido Qubein, entrepreneur supreme and now president of his own alma mater, High Point University, agrees with Desi on the powers of faith and belief, as well as the support of family and friends. Nido's experiences and lessons will remove any doubt or excuses that may have been holding you back or depriving you of your victory. Young Nido, at the age of 17, left Lebanon by himself in search of the rewards of a good education, enterprising opportunities of a free society, and a better life. Nido's father died when he was 6, but the words of his mother had created a blueprint for Nido's successes, which are many and diversified. His mother encouraged Nido to walk hand-in-hand and side-by-side with great people, knowing that we become like those people with whom we spend our time.

I had made the same observation of one of my mentors, Jean Houston, who as a 5 year old chatted in Central Park with Teilhard de Chardin, one of the most profound thinkers and authors of all time. Jean had also given the eulogy for Margaret Mead, the renowned anthropologist. Years ago I remember Nido saying, "You can see further from the shoulders of giants." I think you will love the view! Nido also confirmed that we are not victims of our circumstances as much as our choices and that all meaningful change comes from within. Your present circumstances don't determine where you go; they determine where you start. Martha Stewart, the domestic diva, certainly did not let her circumstances and extended stay at Camp Cupcake, the women's prison, dampen her mindset – only her lifestyle. She will draw from her unfortunate circumstances and, without a doubt, come back twice as strong.

Nido states that focus is power and shared an interesting analogy. Steam rising from a boiling pot is unfocused and fades into the atmosphere. Steam surging through a turbine is focused: It will generate electricity and propel locomotives. Light from an ordinary flame is unfocused and flickers impotently, while a laser beam is highly focused light and will cut steel. If you and your business are not focused, your efforts will diffuse into nothing.

Linda Forsythe, the creator of *Mentors Magazine*, would fully agree with Nido's convictions that heroes and mentors are crucial role models that provide insights and impact on our successes. They *influence* us, which Nido believes is the greatest word in the English language. (Since I have recently written a book entitled *Forget Selling* which presents the 12 principles of influence and persuasion, I would certainly agree.) Nido asserts that we can make a difference by focusing more on our being – who I am determines what I do. As we transcend from success, which is secular and tactile, to significance, which is spiritual and transformational, we expand our personal boundaries and impact the world. Donald Trump claims the winnings of personal success, while Princess Diana and Mother Teresa make a difference in the lives of others. It is our choice.

As we go beyond competence and develop an inner strength, confidence, and charisma, we begin to have impact and influence. Nido shared that his purpose in life is to help others discover their potential and fulfill their life's purpose, which is the most meaningful success we can achieve. Truly, an aimless life is a miserable life.

Seeds of Greatness

Nido refused to answer my question whether champions are made or born. He believes that each one of us is born with a seed of greatness and it is our responsibility to nurture it and make it grow. He also noted that leaders come in all different shapes and forms. For example, an introverted researcher, not the stereotypic, charismatic leader, could discover a new medical breakthrough and lead the world in humanity's health. He emphasized that we all must find our passion and lose ourselves in it, which is what I have witnessed as a common thread in all people of greatness. After all, how can anyone do their best and be a peak performer when they have no interest in what they are doing. Without enthusiasm, a robot can do it better!

A few last words of wisdom from the reflections of Nido are that we need to view hard work as a blessing. I have always wondered when *work* became a dirty word. Here are a few suggestions from Nido's success list:

1. Learn something new everyday and continually improve.
2. Give more than you receive – not just money – but intangibles such as encouragement, love, support, and time.
3. Read everyday – especially the works of great people.
4. Get along with others; it is crucial to success.
5. Develop good habits – habits have more power than desire or belief.
6. Be persistent and prepared for struggles and adversity.
7. Don't waste time – make it count.
8. Be a good steward and contribute to the greater good. Spend 1/3 of your time learning; 1/3 earning; and 1/3 returning.
9. Never retire – redirect. Discover another worthwhile cause.
10. Dwell in possibilities (they are unlimited).

Although Nido was one of my briefer interviews, I had six packed pages of life's lessons, indicating that he does make every minute count. In addition to his active schedule as a speaker, author, consultant, board member, owner of Great Harvest Bread, and university president, Nido is the founder of the Qubein Foundation, which has raised three million dollars to help six hundred students prosper from his ingenuity and generosity.

Building Bridges-Creating Wells-Igniting Fires

Nido stated that his reward is knowing he has helped others by being a vehicle for the common good. His life is about building bridges for people to travel on their life's way, creating wells from which people may drink, and igniting fires to warm people and correct society's ways. Those are certainly selfless goals, although as we give to others we get so much more in return.

In reviewing the core elements of winners, it is not only that they all have high self-esteem and love themselves, they also love others, love what they do, and very simply love life. They all seem more aware of their blessings rather than their obstacles. Nothing gets in their way and nothing holds up progress, but simply slows things down temporarily while they reflect on the lessons learned to bounce back even stronger. Winners never use the word "rejection," which truly is a figment of our imagination and how we choose to perceive events. The word "failure" is also never, ever spoken.   Instead, there is only feedback, corrections, improvements, and lessons to be learned. Although some were poor and penniless or alone in the world and without a supportive environment, they never expressed even an inkling of defeat, which is like cursing in the face of champions.   Instead, they see only new opportunities to learn, explore, and renew. Perhaps when God closes a door, He really does open a window.

There is, however, a strong preference for the word "challenge," which does not threaten nor intimidate but rather excites and entices, charms and seduces them into a forward action mode. Many actually created their own challenges to stimulate what seemed to be somewhat of an addiction to the adrenalin or juices released at the opportunity of one more challenge. In fact, some may have become dependent on this internal, natural high and exhibited symptoms of withdrawal when they had overcome the obstacles, climbed the mountain, and reached the top. Could that possibly have been why Vince Lombardi left his beloved five-time NFL champion team, the Green Bay Packers, for a bottom of the barrel team, the Washington Redskins? Perhaps Michael Jordan had temporarily left basketball to challenge himself with a trial run at baseball for the same reason. Since statistics indicate many CEOs have ADD (Attention Deficit Disorder), perhaps their disorder or curse is also their blessing in that their intolerance for boredom may be the driving force to climb the highest mountains.

There Is No Try – There Is Only Do

Champions also were not only more aware of what they could do rather than what they might not do. They had a definitive forward focus. They seemed more aware and appreciative of life itself and were committed to live each moment of every day to the fullest. They very simply sipped and savored life, lived in the now, and had an incredibly dynamic interaction with life and the lives of others. There was a higher level of energy exchange and a give-and-take approach to life. Having a strong sense of direction toward a defined goal, there was always a clear vision that had meaning and purpose with compelling action. None were really "normal," but then how could one be *ordinary* and accomplish extraordinary things? Many admitted that they knew they were different than their peers at a very early age. Although often seen as eccentric by others, winners simply march to their own drummer.

Their emotional independence allowed them to weather the disapproval of others without compromising their own beliefs and goals. While sensitive to others and cooperative, there was little concession on their commitment to their dreams and desires which were first and foremost, often being willing to sacrifice their own lives if need be. While they had optional plans to achieve their goals, giving up was never an option. There was no escape hatch. They were willing to pay the price and do whatever it might take, but in their own view they were just doing what needed to be done. Their mantra might be, "if you can't, you must – if you must, you can." As Yoda from *Star Wars* so succinctly put it: "There is no try… there is only do!"

Goethe, the German poet, expressed the commitment of champions as follows:

> *Until one is committed, there is hesitancy*
> *The chance to draw back, always ineffectiveness…*
> *The moment one definitely commits*
> *Oneself, then Providence moves too.*
> *All sorts of things occur to help one that*
> *Would never otherwise have occurred. A whole*
> *Stream of events issues from the decision, raising*
>
> *In ones favor all manner of unforeseen incidents and*
> *Meetings and material assistance, which no man could*
> *Have dreamed have come his way.*
> *Whatever you can do or dream, you can begin it. Boldness has genius,*
> *Power and magic in it.*
>
> *Begin it now.*

Getting Back Up to Get the Gold

Bonnie St. John, a Paralympic skier in Austria, 1984, made a most insightful comment. Bonnie mentioned that although she had actually skied faster, a German skier had taken the gold. Here is the lesson to be learned by all. There was as patch of ice where most of the skiers had fallen. Some quit and others got up and finished the race with hopes of still placing. Bonnie was one of the few to get back up, but the German skier returned to her feet faster. The lesson for all of us is that it may not be how fast you ski the race or achieve your goals. The true victory goes to those who get back up or bounce back the fastest. I don't believe bouncing back is determined as much by physical stamina but by emotional endurance and psychological hardiness. It is more about sustaining our sense of hope when in the realms of defeat. Paul Hamm is also a prime example of never giving up hope. After his disappointing performance in the 2004 Olympics in Greece, when everyone but Paul had thrown in the towel, he bounced back to grab the gold. Whether it is Erik Weihenmayer climbing Mt. Everest with no eyes to see—a mind-boggling feat—or Nick Irons swimming the 1,550 miles of the Mississippi River to raise money to fight his father's disease, multiple sclerosis, the lessons shared are not only enlightening, but also rekindle the human spirit within.

Doing Whatever It Takes

There are several common traits that winners seem to share. Whether that person is an Olympian or top athlete, CEO, spectacular musician, or world-changing humanitarian, there was no exception to one trait. They were all people of action and did what must be done. For some it was internally driven such as a personal dream, calling, vision, passion, or strong desire, whether it was simply to survive, overcome obstacles to achieve desired goals, or to serve humankind. A mourning widow of a soldier killed in Iraq said her husband had felt it was his duty to serve. "It was in his blood to serve." Although it was always an internal force that initiated the momentum, the motivations varied by individual values. For example, Mother Teresa and Donald Trump were both very successful in accomplishing their desired goals. However, Mother

Teresa's ambitions were not for power, fame, or fortune, as were Donald Trump's, but rather the internal rewards of making a difference in the lives of those most in need.

The discipline for many is not a challenge but rather a natural by-product of one's need to experience his or her own self-proclaimed freedom as a spiritual transformation. More than beating the odds, it is rising above the odds. That escalation of the soul, a full and honest expression of one's self and one's unfolding of optimal potential is the natural high, the intoxication, and the positive addiction of winning that keeps the fires burning and the willingness to sacrifice and do whatever it takes. It is what compelled Aron Ralston to cut off his own hand when an 800-pound boulder fell on it and trapped him literally *Between A Rock And A Hard Place*, which is also the title of his book. It is the same life force that brought Deena Kastor back to the Olympics time after time after time, to finally win her much-deserved medal – bronze, but in gold plating. Deena confessed it was never her burning desire to be the best, but simply the best she could be.

As You Serve... You Deserve

A few final observations of all the winning people interviewed was that no matter how great the challenge or loss, they always felt a sense of choice, rather than a victim of circumstances. Obviously, the actor Christopher Reeve had definite physical limitations after becoming a quadriplegic. However, he refused to waste time and energy with self-pity on what could have been or should not have been, but rather moved forward with choices to positively shape his future. Miraculously, with sheer determination, will power, and prayer (God power), Christopher chose to make miracles and beat the medical odds by regaining sensation, movement, and his olfactory sense. Many miracles are a manifestation of conscious choices we make. As Henry Ford so very well said, "Whether you think you can or you can't...either way you're right."

The catastrophe of 9/11 certainly demonstrated that we are all champions and can rise to the occasion: if we must, we can! In spite of the tragic choices of the terrorists, many others made brave, heroic choices. Even when it was evident to the passengers of United Flight 93 that there was little or no choice for their own survival, there was incredible spontaneous, strategic planning on the part of Todd Beamer and many others who very quickly created a high performance team that saved the lives of hundreds, perhaps thousands, had they not brought that plane down in a barren field. It was certainly a choice that served, not themselves, but others.

One last thought pattern of all champions was that although humble and sometimes surprised, they felt deserving of their greatness and success no matter what the circumstances of the environment from which they had come. One of the affirmations I encourage my coaching clients to repeat daily is, "I see myself as a basic miracle and worthy of being loved." With a positive belief in not only what you might achieve, but also in what you deserve, you eliminate the self-sabotage that has destroyed the possibilities of so many potential peak performers. As you serve, you deserve. The word "deserve" comes from two Latin words. "De" means "from" and "servire" means "to serve." Abraham Lincoln claimed, "The very best way to help the poor was to not become one of them." Zig Ziglar, "Mr. Motivation" and author of several books on achievement and success states, "The more we help others get what they want, the more they will help us get what we want." Our relationships with others are clearly synergistic. It may be lonely at the top, but rarely does anyone reach the top alone.

If You Think You Are Beaten....

If you think you are beaten you are.

If you think you dare not, you don't

If you try to win, but you think you can't, it is almost certain you won't

If you think you'll lose, you're lost,
For out of the world we find
Success begins with (one's) will
It's all in the state of mind

If you think you are outclassed, you are

You've got to think high to rise
You've got to be sure of yourself before
You can ever win a prize

Life's battles don't always go to the
Stronger or faster (person), but
Sooner or later the (person) who wins
Is the Person who thinks they can

Think and Grow Rich
Napoleon Hill

CHAPTER TWO

FROM SUCCESS TO SIGNIFICANCE: MISSIONS THAT MOTIVATE

> *"Never believe that a few caring people can't change the world. For indeed, that's all who ever have."*
> **Margaret Mead**

We are not put into this world to see what we can get out of it, but rather to see what we can contribute to it to make it better than when we inherited it.

It is almost twenty years since psychologist Charles A. Garfield revealed his findings in his best selling book, *Peak Performers*. Garfield found six attributes shared by peak performers and high achievers:

1. Missions that motivate: the call to action, the "click" that starts things moving.
2. Results in real time: purposeful activity directed at goals that contribute to a mission.
3. Self-management through self-mastery: the capacity for self-observation and effective thinking.
4. Team building/team playing: the complement to self-management – empowering others to produce.
5. Course correction: mental agility, concentration, finding and navigating a "critical path."
6. Change Management: anticipating and adapting to major change while maintaining momentum and balance in an overall game plan.

They are people in process and not infallible heroes, and in many cases they are only a stride or two ahead of the rest of us. These

19

peak performers have no guaranteed strategies for winning, but rather an uncanny knack for increasing the odds in their favor through the use of the skills and attributes we will examine in this book. They act with unusual consistency, with an iron determination and a basic sense of mission.

Fight for Your Limitations and They Are Yours

With all of the people interviewed there was no escape hatch. Although the course or direction may vary, as there was always a backup plan in place, there was never the option of quitting. In fact, options were seen as the core of new opportunities. Winners don't talk about trying, but only what must be done. It is never a question of what can or cannot be done, but only an awareness of personal strengths and what needs to be done. As Richard Bach explained in his wonderful book *Illusions*, "Fight for your limitations and sure enough they're yours." Winners not only think BIG and dwell in possibilities, they also have a forward focus. To "not do" is never an option, which is why champions are consistent and persistent. Brian Tracy, another author and speaker on success, says you take a number and if you stand in line long enough, your number will eventually come up. Unfortunately, most people are just doing a test drive and continually change lines or are too quick to drop out of line when the line seems too long. Then there are those who have never quite figured out what line they are in!

Winners seem to be so completely absorbed in the process that their obsession seems to give their passion roots. Many social change agents have been inspired by personal misfortunes when family members or close friends have become the victims of hideous acts. Mothers Against Drunk Drivers (MADD) and The Amber Alert are examples of massive positive change resulting from tragedy. Samantha Runnion's mother has made a commitment to protecting the lives of other young children from the rape and murder suffered by her own daughter. It is obvious that we are all on this earth for a reason whether we have discovered it or not, and our attempt to feel some consolation is to know that victims have not lived and died without serving a purpose. That purpose may be the instigation of societal change. Certainly Rosa Park's courage to refuse her seat on the bus upon the demand of an entitled white man gave permission for all disempowered people to see some light and to feel some hope.

The United States is a country of mavericks as it was founded by those who challenged the existing order and were willing to fight for their cause of freedom and justice for all, although we too have violated that oath in discovering our own truth. Unfortunately, missions are also a strong, powerful driving force for those with evil intentions, as energy is neutral and does not have a moral code of ethics deciphering what deserves the fruits of its focus. The terrorists who destroyed more than 3,000 innocent lives on September 11, 2001, are an example of the driving force of mission. The savagery of terrorists who brutally took the lives of men, women, and so many small children in Beslan, Russia, just three years later in September, 2004, again exemplifies how evil missions can also overcome the odds and achieve desired goals.

For other heroes, it was a matter of being in sync with their instincts or manifesting their soul's code which is more motivated by internal rewards. Such people are exemplified by Mother Teresa, Princess Diana, philanthropists, volunteers, and the kind souls who put their change in the red kettles of the Salvation Army. In big ways and small ways, it is our personal desire to make a difference and to make our life matter.

Although we often perceive mission as being the same as having a dream or vision, there is a difference at the core of what motivates us. While a dream engages mental images either subconsciously or by conscious wishful thinking, a mission is more of a directed function or task, often with a specific goal for a meaningful reason.

Questions Shape Our Destiny

Nick Irons, the author of Swim Lessons, is an excellent example of someone who achieves extraordinary things, to not just fulfill a dream but to act because of a purposeful reason or cause, which was to raise money for multiple sclerosis, the disease his father had lived with for more than twenty years. Nick felt compelled to do something, rather than to just feel powerless in watching his father's slow but steady loss of freedom and function. For over a decade he has asked himself the question, "What can I do?" This is a crucial factor in manifesting our mission, dreams, and destiny. We must first ask the question. Gandhi said, "If you don't ask – you don't get."

Questions truly shape our destiny and the quality of our questions will determine the quality of our lives. Questions also trigger the brain into a search 24/7 for the answer to our questions. When we ask questions it engages all our faculties into an active pursuit. There is a sequence to the questioning process which is to first ask "what" questions to stimulate visionary, big-picture thinking. Next ask "why" questions which reveal the purpose and thus propels action. The last question to ask is "how" the process can be done and requires more technical organizational skills. Asking a "how" question first often times dampens possibility thinking, idea generation, and innovation.   As a parent, you should be asking your children questions rather than complaining that they ask too many questions. One can never ask too many questions if they truly are seeking answers. The simple question that we often ask children, although not often enough, is: "What do you want to be when you grow up." This automatically plants the seeds of creating a future and confirms that there is one! My question to you is, "What would you be doing if you knew you couldn't fail?"

Inspiration Is Subtle

Inspiration comes to us at unexpected moments and often in subtle ways. It does not hit us over the head with a club, but rather whispers to us gently and may be in disguise. It is our responsibility to be open and listen. Intuitive intelligence (the other IQ) is the essence of my first book, *Why Cats Don't Bark*, and in my interviews with winners, it was clear that they all have a keen sixth sense - intuition. For Nick, the light bulb went on when he was flying over the Mississippi River and realized that the moving waters below were his answer. On June 1, 1997, at the age of 25, Nick plunged into the fifty-six degree water of the Mississippi River in Minneapolis, Minnesota, and took the first of over a million strokes down the 1, 550 mile swim of 118 days, swimming through ten states five hours a day for six days a week. Nick was the second person in history to swim more than 1,550 miles down the muddy, polluted, wavy waters of the Mississippi River and the first to accomplish the feat with the locks and dams of its "modern" form.

Like so many champions Nick too had financial woes, with both his electricity and gas turned off at one point and his car repossessed. However, financial bankruptcy is a temporary state for those who never give up their dream or lose their empowering belief in themselves. After raising hundreds of thousands of dollars for the Multiple Sclerosis Foundation, Nick sought the lure of challenge once again and ventured out on a short bike ride of 10,000 miles along the scenic route of the United States, paddling from the west to east coast.

As a psychotherapist, I have observed that we will often times do more for others than for ourselves. Nick's determination and commitment to make a difference in his father's life certainly validates my observation. The lessons Nick has learned will hopefully provide you with a blueprint for turning your mission into magic:

Discover a Compelling Idea
A dream begins as an idea that won't leave you alone. It can come from anywhere, at any time, and surprise you in curious ways. Infiltrating your thoughts, your idea may show up once a year, once a week, or every minute. Like an insistent child, it refuses to be ignored.

Write Down Your Dream
Writing a dream in vivid detail, as a powerful and heartfelt story, provides the inspiration you need to make your dream come true. You will read and reread your words often. With the excitement they generate, you'll never wonder why you're in that ocean, building that house, or writing at midnight. You'll always know what you're accomplishing.

Make a Plan
A master plan, filled with the details of your journey, will guide you toward your destination. Whether it's scribble on a napkin, laid out in great detail on a spreadsheet, or stored in the compartments of your mind, a plan gives you direction. You'll always know where you're going and how to get there.

Have Fun

Although many dreams have "serious" outcomes, to succeed in completing your goal you have to love what you're doing, have fun, and laugh a lot. Having fun helps you swim a long river, explore the deepest cave, or gaze through a microscope for hours on end. Laughter keeps you stay sane and happy along the way to making your dream come true.

Adjust Your Goals

Big dreams are powerful. They give you a reason for getting up in the morning. They can also be overwhelming. Try breaking a larger goal into smaller pieces and then string the pieces together. Attach rewards to your goals to entice you to complete them. Decide what goals are working and keep them; abandon those that aren't.

Discover Self Confidence

With unlimited self-confidence anything is possible. An unwavering belief in yourself, your talents, and your strengths, enables you to complete your dream. Confidence allows you to turn "you can't" into "I did." You will be tested, but when you forge ahead your confidence soars.

Find Your Motivation

There will be times in the pursuit of your dream when you want to quit. There may be times every day when you want to quit. Without something powerful to keep you going, in good times and bad, you'll find an excuse to say "enough." You may have to remind yourself, from time to time, why you're working so hard to make your dream come true.

Put Together a Great Team

The success of your dream will hinge on the quality and passion of the members of your team. Surround yourself with people who believe in you and believe in your dream. With loyal supporters to lend a hand or cheer you on, accomplishing your dream is easier and more fun

Be Flexible

Every dream is filled with the unknown. In uncharted waters, flexibility moves you over, around or through any obstacle with ease. You can make a split-second decision or find the perfect solution and never look back. Even when you don't know what's around the next bend, going with the flow will ease you toward your destination.

Be Creative

From beginning to end, creativity is at the core of every dream. Creativity brings an idea to life and keeps it breathing. With creativity, good times become great times and problems have solutions. Anything is possible.

In his book *Swim Lessons*, Nick shares his experience in living detail and also provides exercises to help you kick your dream into action.

Powerful Expectations Make Success Inevitable

Being a black belt in Tae Kwon Do, Master Kang Seok Lee, or K.S., has literally "kicked" all his dreams into action. Tae Kwon Do taught Master K.S. Lee many lessons in winning. Kang Seok Lee had $75.00 to his name and no bed to sleep upon, but now has three well-established academies in North Carolina. K.S. agreed with other immigrants interviewed that coming to America with powerful expectations made his success inevitable. When teaching children and adults honor, respect, confidence, and discipline, K.S.'s passion for the martial arts splashes all over you. He confirmed that until he dies, he will wear his uniform—with the black belt I'm sure.

K.S. is a global mentor who truly has the heart of Mother Teresa and the soul of Gandhi. In his effort for his students to realize that they are citizens of the world, K.S. provides cultural exchanges with the Soviet Union, Korea, and other countries. By developing character, inner strength, and global responsibility in his students, Mr. Lee is leveraging his influence to improve society. Seeing children as a family's treasure and hope for the future, K.S. is determined to open every Pandora's box.

From training Tae Kwon Do in the Korean army to volunteering those same services to U.S. troops training for Operation Desert Storm, K.S. cannot stand to sit on the sidelines. Whether it is organizing a benefit for the Make-A-Wish Foundation, instilling self-respect in troubled kids, or restoring self-image to those with disabilities, Mr. Lee never ceases to create new ways to give more and change the way the world thinks.

Success Is Between the Ears

Juanell Teague also changes the way the world thinks transforming speakers into experts by discovering their "knowing" spirit which, if we listen, gives us both direction and the courage to go for it. Whatever it takes to be a champion may not be taught in the classroom. Juanell, who still does not have a high school diploma, coaches Ph.D.'s who come to her for guidance and to get some heart-speak.

Changing the way charities think, Larry Benet, CEO of Outside the Box Promotions, states that success is between the ears and explains it with a simply formula:

Innate Talent + Focused Discipline x Perseverance = Success

It is all about taking the high road and going to a higher playing field, which getting fired allowed him to do. Our eyes are our projectors and thus we see further as we think more deeply.

Mark Johnson, President of Camouflage Communications, has always taken the high road. The author of *How to Get Anyone to Follow You Anywhere*, states a winner must meet the following criteria: "Your actions make a significant, positive impact on human lives and not only your own, but the individuals you have 'touched.' You also become contributors to society in a profound manner." Mark feels winners are compassionate leaders who care, with a capital "C." A well decorated Green Beret officer, Mark knows that no matter what the sacrifice or the price to pay, it is all about doing the right thing. Mark encourages all of us to ask the question: "If it were not for_____, I would not be who I am today or doing what I am doing." In that sense, winners never die but live on in those they have impacted and made a significant difference. (You might consider sending that person a thank you note.) The search for significance is often misdirected and does not always serve society well. For example, graffiti and violence is a gang member's way of having impact and being remembered by the destructive legacy they leave. More people know Al Capone than the current vice president, and maybe even the president, who often speaks of how he hopes to be remembered as well. All of us in our own way wish to pass something on and leave our mark, even if it is just our favorite recipe. How do you wish to be remembered and what changes will you commit to for that to happen. How much time do you have? According to American writer, Henry David Thoreau, "The price of anything is the amount of life you are willing to pay for it."

Turn Your Passion into Your Payday

Greg Reid, author of *The Millionaire Mentor* and founder of Work$mart, Inc., warns people to beware of negaholics who may keep you "grounded" like an anchor, and that the best way to improve your environment may be to change the five people with whom you associate. Greg suggests that you choose your friends wisely. You tend to become the five people you hang out with, and the average of their incomes will be yours. Greg emphasizes believing in your "why" which automatically perpetuates persistence and allows people to turn their passion into their payday. Taking action to dissipate fears is encouraged by his following anecdotes.

> *Where could you be tomorrow if you put your ideas into action today?*
> *Dreams are realities on which you haven't yet taken ACTION.*
> *Never give up! The only two times you need to keep pushing on are: when you want to and when you don't!*
> *Before you can even hope to reach a goal, you first need to HAVE one.*
> *The difference between just TRYING to do something and actually doing it is found in the OUTCOME.*
> *A DREAM written down with a date becomes a GOAL. A goal broken down becomes a PLAN. A plan backed by ACTION makes your dream come true.*
> *The best leaders begin their quests by being the best followers.*

Action dissipates our fears and truly is the bridge between our internal world of thoughts, goals, and intentions, and the results, success, and wealth we enjoy. The choice is yours.

Ellie Drake, founder of Brave Heart Productions, moved to America from Iran to make her dreams come true. Ellie recalled living in fear when bombs from Baghdad were hitting Iran. She mentioned that in Iran 99% of students go to school, considering it a supreme privilege to get an education. What a contrast to the schools in Texas that bribe their students to attend school by rewarding their attendance with money, laptop computers, and even new cars. What happens when our opportunities and freedoms are so abundant that we are blind to their value and have no desire to cash in? Ellie feels when your burning desire, passion, and purpose are nourished and made strong, all fears diminish. Truly, an obstacle is something that you see only when you take your eyes off the goal.

A 12 year-old boy from South Africa had his eyes open to opportunities but having AIDS became an insurmountable obstacle. With wisdom beyond his years, he suggested the following before passing on:

Do all that you can

With what you have

Wherever you are

With the time that you have

CHAPTER THREE

VISIONEERING:
THE POWER OF A DREAM:

*"The future belongs to those who believe
in the beauty of their dreams."*
Eleanor Roosevelt

Truly it is the dreamers who are our survival. Economist John Maynard Keynes, whose ideas so profoundly influenced economic theory and practices in the twentieth century, insightfully stated, "The difficulty lies not so much in developing new ideas as in escaping the old ones." If you value popularity over good thinking, then you will severely limit your potential to excel and go beyond. To be a champion, it is crucial for you to challenge the norm and accept becoming unpopular. In his book *Thinking for a Change,* John C. Maxwell clarifies the woes of popular thinking as I have listed below:

> *Too Average to Understand the Value of Good Thinking*
> *Too Inflexible to Realize the Impact of Changed Thinking*
> *Too Lazy to Master the Process of Intentional Thinking*
> *Too Small to See the Wisdom of Big-Picture Thinking*
> *Too Satisfied to Unleash the Potential of Focused Thinking*
> *Too Traditional to Discover the Joy of Creative Thinking*
> *Too Naïve to Recognize the Importance of Realistic Thinking*
> *Too Undisciplined to Release the Power of Strategic Thinking*
> *Too Limiting to Feel the Energy of Possibility Thinking*
> *Too Trendy to Embrace the Acceptance of Popular Thinking*

Too Proud to Encourage the Participation of Shared Thinking
Too Self-absorbed to Experience the Satisfaction of Unselfish Thinking
Too Uncommitted to Enjoy the Return of Bottom-Line Thinking

A New Idea Is Delicate

Maxwell also encourages reflective thinking to give emotional integrity to your thought life by enabling you to distance yourself from the intense emotional charge from various experiences and see them with fresh eyes. Reflective thinking allows you to examine tragedies in the light of truth and logic, which often may be painful and thus denied or blinding. Andy Sefanovich, the cofounder of Play, a company that fosters creativity, advises people to become more creative by building a creative community, and demystifying creativity as a special gift of the chosen few. His recommendation is simply that people look at more stuff and think about it harder to cultivate their own personal creativity.

Since creativity tends to be contagious, it is important that we all hang around other creative people who energize, inspire, and take our ideas to another level. Try brainstorming with a bunch of geniuses and watch your creative juices flow! Remember, you can always see further from the shoulders of giants. Perhaps the only way to get out of our box is to get into someone else's, but before we can break out of our box, we must first discover what box we are in. In other words, know thyself! David Hill says, "Studies of creativity suggest that the biggest single variable of whether or not employees will be creative is whether they perceive they have permission." Charlie Brower asserts, "A new idea is delicate. It can be killed by a sneer or a yawn; it can be stabbed to death by a quip and worried to death by a frown on the right man's brow."

Spontaneity ignites creativity that allows us to expand our mental boundaries, think big, become visionary, and create our dreams. As Maxwell comments, "A creative environment promotes the freedom of a dream. A creative environment encourages the use of a blank sheet of paper and question, 'If we could draw a picture of what we want to accomplish, what would it look like?' (Note that again the catalyst for our creative juices is asking a question.) A creative environment allowed Martin Luther King, Jr. to speak with passion and declare to millions, 'I have a dream,' and not 'I have a goal.' Goals may give focus, but dreams give power. Dreams expand the world. That is why James Allen suggested that 'dreamers are the saviors of the world.'" Unfortunately creativity is so often smothered and squelched rather than encouraged and nurtured.

Life Is a Series of Dots We Must Connect

Vince Poscente, a Canadian Olympian, peak performance strategist, and author of *The Ant and the Elephant*, had both a goal and a dream. Vince likened overcoming one's fears and reaching one's goals as being similar to eating an elephant, just one bite at a time. We can turn a 5,000 gallon of water blue with just one drop of dye per day, but you will never notice it. Knowing you can never eliminate risks, but only minimize them, he feels you will never know unless you try, and Vince tries just about everything even if he gets a late start. He started ski racing recreationally at age 26 and in less than four years at age 30 he found himself taking on the slopes in Albertsville, France, in the 1992 Olympics. While Vince did not see himself as being extraordinary as a child, he does recall seeing a politician speaking and deciding he wanted to do that… speak. Describing himself as a nerd at heart, as a "C" student he didn't academically measure up to full-fledged nerd status. He loved sports but was not particularly good. He was OK on the clarinet, but where he excelled was his determination and willingness to do the extra work required once he discovered his truth and his passion.

Fortunately, his mother exposed him to many things, an approach that increases the odds for increased opportunities. He discussed the mathematics of opportunity where if you keep opening new doors, you develop a momentum driving you to the top of whatever mountain you choose to climb or ski. Vince defines life as a series of dots that we must connect, with the random dots being our defining moments or pivotal points.

For example, when Vince was just 16, a close friend, Jill Kudryk, died of a heart attack at age 17. At that moment he decided he would try everything at least once and felt a sense of urgency to experience all the dots and to connect them as well. Taking a year to backpack around the world was a start. The Olympics provided another experience, and he swears that when he dies he will have twenty projects hanging. Other defining moments for Vince were at age 14 watching the opening ceremonies in Montreal on TV, and at age 26 attending the Olympics in Calgary not as a participant, but a spectator. At that moment he vowed to never sit on the sidelines of life ever, ever again.

Vince makes it clear that unless we are in alignment with our core genius and calling, we may fumble and stumble through life, for his attempts at pre-medicine left him with F's and the challenge, which Vince always sees as opportunity, to get back into the university. Life is full of moguls, especially at the Olympics. Skiing at 138 mph, Vince hit a bump and came in 15th rather than getting the gold, but according to Vince, since Canadians don't win as much, they still clap and applaud one's participation and fine effort. Perhaps we in the USA need to recognize that winning is a journey of integrity and fine effort and not only the end result. It is a path to perpetual improvement and an effort in excellence without steroids!

Life's defining moments may be the simple things. Vince recalls being the moderator of his Christmas play in kindergarten as a turning point. I recall getting hooked on performing in kindergarten when I was asked to get in the center of the circle and lead the big K class in a cheer. I had a competitive edge because my older sister was a grade school cheerleader for the mighty Cardinals, and thus I had unlimited mentorship. But like the ski slopes, the ride may get bumpy. Vince's second grade teacher gave him the feeling he was borderline retarded because he daydreamed a lot. He thus withdrew into a self-made shell. (How does one's dream come true if you haven't first dreamed the dream?) Another defining moment, Vince began transcendental meditation at age 14, which initiated a process of ongoing change and growth. While Vince stated he did not see himself as extraordinary as a child, he had extraordinary visions but he just had not yet connected the dots.

Intoxicated by the Challenge

Another mind-boggling dream was fulfilled when the blind mountain climber, Eric Weihenmayer, of Denver, Colorado, topped Mount Everest. Come on, a blind man climbing the big one! Clear vision obviously has very little to do with 20/20 eyesight, but rather is a reflection of an ever-expanding, unlimited mindset, or what I define as MindShift. Blind since the young age of 13, Weihenmayer lost his sight to a rare disease called retinoschisis. In spite of what many would consider a legitimate limitation, Erik only looked to his dreams, realizing that he may have to be more creative, do things differently, and think out of the box to accomplish his goals. After all, an obstacle is something you see only after you take your eyes off your goal. Being blind did not allow young Erik to *see* presumed obstacles, which may have been a blessing in disguise. Perhaps we all need to become temporarily blinded of our *perceived* obstacles.

Erik, an obviously introspective and spiritual man with wisdom beyond his years, seemed to have a strong sense of identity when he stated, "You're a climber first and a blind person second." How often might you define yourself not by your true identity, goals, and aspirations, but rather by your self-imposed mental and emotional limitations? I mentioned Erik being introspective. Perhaps our outward sight may actually distract us from seeing the deeper vision that lies within us. Erik also is a perfect example of our body's ability to adapt and compensate for areas where we are weak or without talent. He also illustrates how little we use the gifts and unlimited potential available but so rarely developed or utilized. Erik reports that although not being able to see the path before him, he used his sense of hearing, listening to footsteps around him, and a bell tied to the climber ahead of him.

Not only has Erik accomplished the 29,035 foot peak, but in 1995 he scaled North America's highest peak, Mount McKinley, and in 1997 he topped Mount Kilimanjaro, and in January 1999, he climbed Argentina's Aconcagua, the tallest mountain in South America. By the way, Erik loves diversity and thus is also a certified sky and scuba diver, as well as a competitor in long distance biking and marathon running, skiing, and mountaineering. Erik has no excuses, what are yours? I would guess Eric would agree that before you can become really good at something, you have to be willing to accept being bad.

Erik's insights and experiences so well describe the MindShift of winners and champions. As Nido Qubein mentioned, "We don't retire, we just redirect." While Erik realized that he could never run down the basketball court or catch a pop fly, rather than pout and whine, he simply redirected his talents and energies to what he could do. Erik learned to dwell in possibilities. *The Boston Channel* reports many of Erik's experiences which represent so many of the extraordinary people I had interviewed.

Intoxicated by the challenge, Erik reported, "It's like you know you're doing something that human beings shouldn't be doing, you know?" While we need not deify winning, perhaps the "high" of winning does elevate us in a way that in stretching our human abilities and busting the barriers of perceived limitations, we do experience the power of something much, much greater than ourselves. I have written this book as human permission to remove your personal blinders and expand your own vision of possibilities. With so many being blind to their untapped potential, hopefully if this guy can climb the big one without sight, you will relinquish your excuses from walking up a few steps.

Erik also recalled in his interview with *The Boston Channel,* "You're not thinking about the fact that you're blind, you're just thinking about what you've got to do with your brain and your body." Winners are so totally engaged in their goals that they actually *lose sight* of any internal or external hindrance or roadblock. We all have just so much energy and to the degree that we are 100% positive, there can be no negativity. (You do the math.) Where you choose to direct that energy is just that...your choice!

Flow and "In The Zone"

My first book, *Why Cats Don't Bark,* reveals that we all have a soul's code or calling, based on Harvard research as reported in James Hillman's book, *The Soul's Code.* I had also sited research from the book *Flow* by Mihaly Csikszentmihalyi of the University of Chicago. Peak performers are people who are in sync with their instincts and thus experience a personal alignment with their core genius, creating the powerful state of "flow." It is a state of perfect balance between boredom and anxiety when our efforts seem effortless, purposeful, and timely. Flow is triggered by challenges, which seem to be the breakfast of champions.

Erik reported, "It was so tactile, so totally engaging, I couldn't imagine doing anything else." Does this not reflect the same experience of "flow" when Michael Jordan scored the winning point so effortlessly in the final second, leaving the Utah Jazz in despair. Being "in the zone" provides Tiger Woods with the same pleasure, optimal performance, and income!

When Sarah Hughes earned her well-deserved gold medal at the Winter Olympics 2000 in Utah, her skating performance made "flow" appear to be an out-of-the-body experience. It was as if the young 16 year old was in spirit only, for she appeared to be without any body weight as she swirled and soared above the ice. Sarah is the ultimate example of the power of a dream or wish without a doubt. There must be more than hope, as Desi Williamson stated, there must be a belief and certainty. More than positive thinking, there must an internal "knowing" that the miracles in our minds will manifest.

As a psychotherapist, I have been aware of how much of mental health has to do with "control." Certainly feeling out of control creates a frightening feeling of powerlessness and helplessness, which is why rape, the loss of a loved one, or loss of a relationship can be so devastating. We feel out of control simply because we cannot control the situation. The paradox of my work with eating disorders, such as anorexia nervosa, is that the more anorexics attempt to be "in control," the more out of control they become in that by severely controlling their intake of calories, they lose control of their health and their lives.

Connecting with a Higher Power

Perhaps that sense of overcoming and regaining control is one of the ultimate human experiences as best described by Erik in an interview with *CNN/Sports Illustrated*, "I want to summit, and I like the pioneering aspect of being first. For me, though, the process is more fun, the moments of bliss that connect you with who you are. The summit is just a symbol that on that day you brought an uncontrollable situation under control." Perhaps our feeling of being more alive is contingent upon our awareness of our power and strength to overcome and beat the odds. I cannot emphasize enough that it is *awareness* that is core to the joy and happiness we experience. Not the experience, but our *awareness* of what is and who we are is the crucial factor that seems to be heightened when we connect with a greater force or higher power than ourselves.

People report a heightened awareness of being connected to a higher power in their prayers. Others may find their communion with nature creates that same sense of being connected to a greater whole. I am a strong believer in the philosophy of the martial arts in that to overcome we must always "go with" the opposing force. That concept was validated by Erik's comment, "You don't conquer a mountain, you work with it. You sneak up on it when it takes a nap. If you don't abide by the rules, you get crushed. I like that. I like to feel I'm part of nature, not separate from it." Most importantly of all in the enlightening interview with *Sports Illustrated* were Erik's comments on how to experience the real beauty of life, which is what makes all of us winners. "I like the spiritual feeling of being on a mountain. The space. The sounds. The vast openness of it. The most annoying question I get is, 'Why climb when I can't see the view from the top?' You don't climb for the view. No one suffers the way you do on a mountain for a beautiful view. The real beauty of life happens on the side of the mountain, not the top." I think that sums it up and says it all.

Every Vision Requires Revision

Once we have achieved our goals, we need to continually renew them and have a revision of our previous vision. The purpose of having a goal is not to so much to reach it, but to give us direction and focus. Having a strategy or plan inspires us to take action and enjoy the pleasure and awareness of the process of a continually evolving and expanding growth experience which is when we are truly most alive. "Don't die until you're dead."

There are several common traits, personal characteristics, and habits that winners seem to share. Whether that person is an Olympian or top athlete, CEO, spectacular musician, or world-changing humanitarian, there was no exception to one trait. They were all people of action and did what must be done. For some it was internally driven such as a personal dream, "calling," or vision; for others it was survival; and then there were those who were passionate about serving humankind and making a difference in the world.   Although it was always an internal force that initiated the momentum, the motivations varied by individual values. For example, Mother Teresa and Donald Trump were both very successful in accomplishing their desired goals. However, Mother Teresa's ambitions were not for power, fame, or fortune, as are Donald Trump's, but rather the internal rewards of making a difference in the lives of those most in need. Clarity of vision certainly attracts success, but clarity of goals often serves as a trigger to focus and ignite the fires.

The Power of a Dream

Dr. Martin Luther King, Jr. knew the power of a dream. Dr. King not only liberated his African-American brothers and sisters but the human spirit and the power of everyone's dream, without limitations of color, creed, or culture. Of all modern day orators and leaders, Martin Luther King certainly would be considered one of the best orators of all time for not only his ability to communicate and convey the dream, but also his ability to strategize and execute that dream.

When he organized the bus boycott, with seventy-five percent of all riders on the Montgomery, Alabama bus system being African-American, the bus system lost money, and raised prices. In their anger the authorities began to bomb the protesters which only united them and made them stronger, using no violence in their protest. Finally, on November 13, 1956, the Supreme Court of the United States ruled Montgomery's segregation laws unconstitutional. The next day Ms. Rosa Parks, along with E.D. Nixon and Martin Luther King, Jr., proudly took their seats in the front of the bus, grinning from ear to ear. These brave souls did not follow the paved path, but courageously went where there was no path and left a trail. Things do take time…and courage.

Cultural behaviors and unspoken beliefs typically change long before people openly concede to each other that times have changed. A new array of choices seems too rich and varied – the promises too open-ended. Our worries are our safe boundaries; over time we have learned to identify with our limits. Often leery of trusting the promise of an oasis, we defend the merits of the desert.

Not More Knowledge but a New Way of Knowing

It is distrust of self that makes people vulnerable and obedient. Our conformity has been due to our fear of ourselves: our doubts about the rightness of our own decisions. We are the future. We are the revolution. Most problems cannot be solved at the level at which they're asked. They must be reframed and put into a larger context. It is not more knowledge, but a new way of knowing. We have not fallen into crisis after crisis because our ideals had failed, but because we had never applied them. We are indeed participants in reality. We are observers who affect what we observe.

Martin Luther King, Jr. so well expressed the spirit of winning in many of his inspiring speeches. In *I Have a Dream,* Dr. King demonstrates hope, optimism, and faith in overcoming the struggles together to reach the summit – freedom:

"This is our hope. This is the faith that I go back to the South with. With this faith we will be able to hew out of the mountain of despair a stone of hope. With this faith we will be able to transform the jangling discords of our nation into a beautiful symphony of brotherhood. With this faith we will be able to work together, to pray together, to struggle together, to stand up for freedom together, knowing that we will be free one day…. Free at last! Free at last! Thank God almighty, we are free at last!"

In the speech he gave the day before he was assassinated, Dr. King seemingly had an intuitive hunch about death being near as he assures his followers, "Like anybody, I would like to live a long life; longevity has its place. But I am not concerned about that now. I just want to do God's will. And He's allowed me to go up to the mountain. And I've looked over. And I've seen the promised land. I may not get there with you." A courageous visionary who feels content and fulfilled because of serving his "calling" or purpose then continues, "And I'm happy tonight, I'm not worried about anything. I'm not fearing any man. Mine eyes have seen the glory of the coming of the Lord."

CHAPTER FOUR

MIND MASTERY:
OPTIMISM IS NOT OPTIONAL

> *"Of all the creatures of earth, man alone is the greatest architect of his destiny. The greatest revolution in our generation is the discovery that human beings, by changing the inner attitudes of their minds, can change the outer aspects of their lives."*
> **William James**

While kids make up their minds, adults have the challenge of changing their minds which is often accompanied by resistance to eliminating old habits. Unfortunately, what you don't fix, your kids inherit. One often wonders if happiness is genetic, learned, or a result of divine intervention. People seem to have different levels of happiness that seem to be independent of their circumstances or environment. Researchers refer to this happy habit as "joy juice."

Nature vs. Nurture

For example, Mother Teresa was always smiling, upbeat, positive, and energetic in spite of living in poverty. Yet others who seem to have it all in terms of wealth, fame, and power often suffer from a quiet desperation that they attempt to resolve with drugs or suicide. In studies where the subjective well-being of fraternal and identical twins were measured, forty to fifty-five percent of SWB (subjective well-being) seemed to be genetic. Thus, being happier might be as futile as trying to be taller. However, if twins shared similar environments even though they grew up apart from each other, there was less variance.

Environment seems to have an accumulative effect and thus became a stronger factor with age.

The conclusion on nature vs. nurture regarding attitude, optimism, and happiness is that it is the unique experiences to which we are exposed and what we make of those experiences that determine our overall level of happiness. We must also distinguish between happiness and pleasure. Pleasure is a more transient experience associated with a specific reward or event and does not lead to happiness if it is inconsistent with or adverse to a person's greater goals. Happiness is a more enduring state related to an overall experience of one's life. Perhaps it is in the absence of overall happiness that people seek it by pleasuring themselves with temporary "highs" such as drugs, alcohol, gambling, pornography, and other unhealthy addictions. We all seem to seek the right answer but perhaps in the wrong places. Knowing that the answers lie within, perhaps taking time out for prayer, introspection, or reflection, will better connect us with the true source of our happiness and joy. In fact, happier, more optimistic people tend to have greater left-over-right PFC (pre-frontal cortex) dominance than less happy people. A Buddhist monk who spent many years practicing the art of meditation had the greatest left-sided dominance in a study by neuroscientist Richard Davidson.

Your pet cat expresses her pleasure in being petted by her purring, and perhaps a dog is a man's best friend because of his responsiveness to the pleasure we provide by simply acknowledging him or giving him the premier seat in our pickup truck. The experience of winning certainly produces pleasure. This is why I strongly encourage parents to involve their children in play and healthy, meaningful activities such as sports, music, drama, or whatever is in sync with their instincts and natural interests. If children experience the pleasure from positive activities they get a bit hooked on it, and thus they will be much more resilient to those who may tempt them with the quick fix and pleasure short-cuts such as drugs, alcohol, violence, and foods loaded with sugar that are also addictive. They also become self-motivated which makes parenting a lot more fun.

Nature's happy drug, beta-endorphin, is released whenever we complete projects and in a sense trains you by rewarding you with the pleasure and the good feeling you receive when you have finished the task. The bigger the job…the bigger the rush of beta-endorphins you get upon completion. Whether it's yard work, a house project, or an assignment at the office, have you ever noticed how you feel so driven to just getting it done and checking it off your list? The endorphins made you do it!

Good things, however, can go bad. It is sad to see how many Olympians have sabotaged their success by their steroid dependency. Apparently their addiction to the pleasure of winning caused them to lose a healthy perspective, as all addictions do, and compromise their integrity and values. As people throughout the world pursue their right to "life, liberty, and the pursuit of happiness," we must decipher between true happiness which is a "do-it-yourself job" based on the purpose-driven life and not a series of quick-trick pleasures.

Optimism vs. Optimal Thinking

Helen Keller reminds us that, "No pessimist ever discovered the secrets of the stars, or sailed to an uncharted land, or opened a new heaven to the human spirit." There is, however, a distinction between optimism, optimal thinking, and learned optimism. In *Learned Optimism,* Dr. Martin Seligman states: "If the cost of failure is high, optimism is the wrong strategy. Sometimes we need to cut our losses and invest elsewhere rather than find reasons to hold on."

In *Optimal Thinking* by Rosalene Glickman, the author also differentiates between optimism and optimal thinking. "Optimal thinkers eliminate unnecessary disappointment because they entertain realistic expectations and focus on optimizing situations within their control… They simply explore their options and make the optimal choice from realistic alternatives. Optimal thinkers embrace reality and ask: 'What's the best thing I can do under the circumstances?'…When evaluating risk, we must weigh the probability and cost of failure (including the ability to cope with the consequences) against the cost and benefits of prevention."

Optimism Is Not Just Improving but Maximizing Potential

Optimism is often lost by shattered dreams. In fact, for some a bitterness and cynicism may have crept in its place. Optimism is not just improving but maximizing all that we have in our given circumstances. It is taking a problem-solving, solution-thinking approach to life which is applied optimism. Certainly Christopher Reeve had to make a few adjustments and very constructively redirected his life's goals and ambitions from being Superman and seemingly invincible to just being able to control and master a simple movement. The winds in our lives can change course in a flash. We therefore must prepare mentally to redirect and overcome our new challenges. Christopher admitted to being very impatient with people who are able-bodied but seem paralyzed by their own volition. Anita Robertson summarizes our choices within the circumstances that challenge us. "Life is like a piano. What you get out of it depends on how you play it."

A month before Christopher passed on he appeared on Oprah Winfrey and stated he thought it was very possible that he would walk again. When she asked what would happen if he did not walk again he said, "Then I won't walk again." Said another way by the revered poet Robert Frost, "It goes on." Nevertheless Reeve's optimism, hope, and determination made him a prime example of the might of indomitable will, as he achieved some movement through sheer desire, determination, and focus. Christopher admitted that his hope decreased after the first five years, but that it actually increased his determination. The actress Lucille Ball had the same philosophy. "One of the things I learned the hard way was it does not pay to get discouraged. Keeping busy and making optimism a way of life can restore your faith in yourself."

Christopher Reeve was obedient to the suggestion of the late Eleanor Roosevelt. "You have to accept whatever comes, and the only important thing is that you meet it with the best you have to give." Life is the music that dances through our days. My plans were to interview Christopher before he died, but obviously circumstances changed for him as it did for over 175,000 people in Asia on a beautiful sunny day on December 26, 2004, when the winds of time changed and the tsunami so swiftly stole so many lives. I now ask you, "How much time do you have?" What do you want to do with the time you have, which with all certainty is only *now*?

The Power of Now

Living in the ever-precious present is well explained in the book, *The Power of Now,* by Eckhart Tolle. In his work Tolle states, "You are here to enable the divine purpose of the universe to unfold. That is how important you are!" Every moment of life is a miracle for us to enjoy and share. Unhappiness and negativity are more contagious than physical diseases, and anything you do in a negative mind state contaminates and spreads ill will, creating a psychic pollution and inner poverty where we may, as Christ put it, "Gain the world, but lose our own soul." We must always make a clear distinction between pleasure, which results from outside causes and events; and joy, an inner state independent of outside circumstances.

Negativity is not a natural state and exists only in human beings (except for our pets that may be contaminated by our neurosis). Have you ever seen a cat with low self-esteem or a lack of confidence? How many dogs hold a grudge when you daily abandon them? The dog holds no grudge, but jumps for joy upon your return. If negative thoughts persist, use them as lessons to learn and as triggers to let go of your resistance. As in the martial arts, we must "go with" or yield to the attacking force to overcome it. As we shift from conditioning to conscious choice, we move out of the darkness and into the light, thus becoming more aware, enlightened, and insightful. We then escape our personal bondage to the negative and experience spiritual freedom.

While we all need to move forward, positive thinking may be a suppression of a negative reality and the denial of a truth that must be accepted and embraced to change, manage, and regain control. If negative thoughts and feelings are not acknowledged and resolved, they continue to grow like a cancer and may destroy our success and personal relationships. Never confuse wishful thinking with reality as it deceives us and gives us a false sense of security. On the other hand, our level of achievement is always compromised if our thinking is less than optimal.

In fact we must look to not merely improve our performance, but to maximize it.

Silence Is The Language of God

Frank Bucaro, author of *Trust Me* and *How to Succeed Ethically When Others Bend the Rules*, is very present and lives in the now. He reminds all of us that knowledge is the "stuff," and wisdom is what you do with it. Drawing his strength from contemplation, prayer, and meditation, Frank now speaks and consults on business ethics, and states he simply took the "God talk" out of his previous role as a theologian and teacher in Catholic schools and colleges.

Frank is on a perpetual vacation and loves to cite Mark Twain: "The goal in life is to make your vocation your vacation." Frank emphasized that we are all called to "become," and that if you aren't better today from what you learned yesterday, you have wasted it. For Frank everyday is Christmas and every night is Thanksgiving: life is one big celebration. He defines winning as when you have done everything you can to live up to your potential and use it for the benefit of others so you can see the fruit that results from your development. This echoes Albert Einstein who said, "We have to do the best we can. This is our sacred human responsibility."

Without a spirit life we are handicapped, for we are all spiritual beings in a human body that must coexist. I have always felt that God is too big for any one religion, and Frank, who has read the Koran and Kabbalah, feels they all have the same roots, perhaps all saying the same thing in different ways. Learning much from Native American writings, Frank sees silence as the language of God and everything less as a power translation. Amen!

Frank continued to explain that you must be what you want others to see and that we all are here to plant seeds that others must water and fertilize for themselves. Frank simply helps people to see life differently, for education only happens when learning links up to people's experiences, which is probably why we remember more of our grade school and high school teachers than our college professors. Who do you remember and why did they leave a lasting impression? What was their point of impact? Although a primary influence on his life, the friar's perception of Frank as a delightful discipline problem caused him to leave the seminary after a couple years of valuable experiences which taught him about *Taking the High Road*, the title of one of his three books.

We Must First Embrace Ourselves

Frank warns that we should not let the world dictate our course and that the world's perception of us should not determine our self-esteem. Instead, our self-esteem should be determined by our perception of ourselves to the world. He warns that this cannot be taught but learned by first embracing ourselves.

Optimism results from gratitude that makes us more aware of the good, the positive, and the blessings in our lives. As I watched the children who survived the recent tsunami receiving very small token gifts from volunteers, I noticed how each one put his or her hands together in a prayer position and gently bowed after receiving the gifts. I was struck by how they were able to focus on this small gesture of giving and caring when they had just lost their homes, perhaps their parents, and even their entire families. I also noted their unbelievable ability to cope with such an overwhelming disaster. Could the optimism and hope witnessed perhaps be a result of the learned attitude of gratitude? What will you do daily to reflect on the blessings that are yours? Trust me, they're there, whether you chose to see them or not.

Frank quoted a Native American Indian Tecumseh who said, "If you see nothing to be thankful for, then the fault lies in yourself." His favorite quote, however, is from LaKota Su. "Remember my children when you were born, you cried and the world rejoiced, but live your life so when you die, the world cries and you rejoice."

Seeing each day as an opportunity and emulating the creed of St. Francis of Assisi, Frank feels all human beings have the obligation, with a capital "O," to develop their gifts, talents, and capabilities to the best of their ability for the betterment of other people and to leave this world a better place. (Some of us have a lot of catching up to do.) Since we all have been called to be a family, we need to "get it right" here on earth. Frank emphasized that without love and health we can do nothing.

To Be a Winner You Must Think Like a Winner

Optimism and a millionaire mind does create wealth according to T. Harv Eker, founder of Peak Potentials Training and author of *Secrets of The Millionaire Mind*. Harv went from zero to millionaire in only 2 ½ years. While lottery winners lose their money almost as fast as they make it, people who have earned billions of dollars seem to get it back as quickly as they lose it. Donald Trump is a perfect example of the financial roller coaster that rebounds as quickly as it hits bottom. The Trump philosophy is very simple. "To be a winner you must think like a winner and never quit."

We all have a financial thermostat or what I refer to as a "success set point." Eighty percent of people never become financially free because they set their expectations way too low and are happy to just pay the bills. If that is your goal, that is as high as you will ever go. It is our inner world of thoughts that determines our outer, real world successes. In other words, our roots determine our fruits. The invisible, such as our unconscious conditioning and thoughts, is the cause of our effects: our financial success and our personal joy.

Winners with wealth feel more in control and know that they create their life, while poor people feel powerless and that "life happens" to them. Those people feeling victimized by life tend to blame others: their boss, taxes, bills, their spouse, and especially their parents. People who are broke rationalize and justify their situation with false assurances such as "money is just not very important to me," and if it is not important to you of course you will not have it. Those who are without continually complain and since what we focus on expands and we thus attract more of, it then becomes a self-fulfilling prophecy. Harv states, "There is no such thing as a rich victim."

We Can Play to Win or Play Not to Lose

Basically we have two choices. We can play to win, offensively, or we can play not to lose, defensively, where we are just happy to pay the bills and merely exist or just hang in there. A frequently learned message for the middle class is, "I just want to be comfortable," which creates a self-limiting set point. If you resent the rich and see them as just lucky or as snobs, you will certainly never be one of them. However, if you admire people such as Roger Clemens, the pitcher for the Houston Astros who signed on for eighteen million dollars, you have the right attitude and intention to attract similar wealth your way. It's simply how natural and universal laws work for those who embrace them. While intentions are on the mental and spiritual plane, actions bridge our inner world with the outer world and create our desired results.

The difference between winners with wealth and those who are struggling is simply that those with wealth move ahead in spite of their fears and refuse to allow doubt and uncertainty to stop them. It is only when we stretch beyond our comfort zone and go beyond what is convenient that we experience the joy of growing. If you're working too hard for too little, you probably need to change your financial blueprint.

A Realist Is a Pessimist in Denial

Author of *The Acorn Principle*, Jim Cathcart, explains the experience of expanding your limits and venturing out of your comfort zone to live more fully. He affirms that our genetic purpose is to grow and live fully, and if we choose not to everyone is cheated. To prevent burnout and create a work-life balance we need to redefine balance and realize that we cannot spin all ten plates at once with equal intensity in sequence. However, we can focus on one at a time and develop a level of focus that will break through barriers and allow us to beat the odds. This system of intermittent attention allows us to go the extra mile. For example during college exam time most of us have to let go of dehydrating our fruits and vegetables and contemplating our navel until semester break.

Jim also cautioned that one of the worst things you can do is to believe you cannot do something and yet continue to persist. Either change your belief system or stop doing it, unless you find pleasure in proving yourself right about your wrongs. Without optimism there can be no action or solutions for who would even attempt to solve a problem or make a difference if they were sincerely convinced their efforts would prove worthless. Motivation and behavior is sustained by our hope of the outcome.

Jim defines a realist as a pessimist who refuses to admit it. In their denial, realists often see a given status as reality rather than seeing beyond and what might be possible. A card-carrying pessimist is one who complains about the noise when opportunity knocks. In contrast, informed optimism is the only creative, productive state of mind that moves us forward and gives us life advances. More than optimism we must always have options and a plan B or backup plan when we leave the safety of our comfort zone. When God closes a door, He opens a window, but we have to notice that the window is open and crawl through.

Genius Is Reading the Mind of God

Jim also emphasized continual self-examination with a personal audit. To know more we must *notice* more and as we notice more options we create more opportunities. Jim referred to a book by Rick Wallace, *The Science of Getting Rich,* and another book written just after the turn of the century by Wallace Wattles, *How to Be a Genius.* Genius is being able to read the mind of God and to see natural patterns and the little details that make the big details. Jim mentioned that the pattern of people moving through LAX, the international airport in Los Angeles, is similar to the patterns of ants. I would agree, as everyone seems to be in an abstract random state of chaos, yet everyone is going somewhere with a specific destination in mind. There are no isolated acts except for momentarily.

Jim added that for true fulfillment there must be a need outside of yourself, for vision without action is hallucination and action without vision is random activity. He referred to Zig Ziglar's story, "You have to prime the pump. Action precedes motivation. You have to prime the pump and get the juice flowing, which motivates you. If you stop, you will have to start all over again. ..." Following through on our goals and visions comes easier when we are not just self-serving but making a difference in another's life.

One of the reasons people don't achieve their dreams is that they desire to change their results without changing their thinking. James Allen, philosopher and author of *As a Man Thinketh,* wrote, "Good thoughts and actions can never produce bad results; bad thoughts and actions can never produce good results." The dance of the spheres has always been an interesting interplay of brainpower and creativity, with both being essential to a winner's formula to success. Winners are creative, resourceful, and solution thinkers. They are not born with bigger brains so to speak, but develop the discipline and desire to maximize their natural gifts and excel in their efforts. They seem to get hooked onto the natural highs of rising above and conquering all.

Optimism Is an Incurable Condition

Dr. Avram Goldstein, director of the Addiction Research Foundation at Stanford University, had discovered the existence of substances in our brains similar to morphine and heroin. Research has located receptor areas in the brain that act as "locks" that only these unknown substances would fit, like "keys." These natural hormonal "keys" include enkephalin, endorphin, beta-endorphin, and dynorphin which are all natural pain relievers more powerful than morphine. In fact, beta-endorphin is fifty times more powerful than morphine, and dynorphin is one hundred and ninety times more potent than morphine. Perhaps optimists, a most common trait in winners, are people high on endorphins! Optimism is an incurable condition in people of faith. People have actually sued for being held just briefly in an investigation because of the emotional damage of being robbed of their innocence. Another way of saying that may be that they were robbed of their optimism, faith, and trust.

The traditional view of achievement needs some serious revision, as it assumes that failure results from lack of talent and desire. Failure, however, can occur when talent and desire are present in abundance but optimism is missing.

The survival of Elian Gonzalez, the young Cuban refugee whose boat capsized in his mother's search for freedom in America, is a prime example of how optimism sustains us. While drifting in the Atlantic Ocean, it may have been Elian's prayers that gave him the hope and optimism to survive until rescued. There are also reports that the dolphins actually protected him from being prey to the hungry sharks, as Elian stated they had lifted his rubber raft above the waters when in danger. The laws of attraction obviously go beyond the human sphere.

Symbols also provide hope and optimism, which is why many of us love to collect artifacts with rainbows and butterflies. Victor Frankl, in his most renowned book, *Mans Search for Meaning,* clearly states that it was his vision of survival and being reunited with his wife that allowed him to survive the Nazis and weather conditions that seemed humanly impossible. Unfortunately, his wife was not spared, but he lived a long, fulfilling life and from his experience he created Logotherapy. Michael Johnson, the US Olympian runner, is known for running in his "gold shoes" that gave him the inspiration to run his best and be deserving of the shoes he wore.

From Stumbling Blocks to Stepping Stones

In the 2004 Olympics in Athens, Deena Kastor was once 18th in the same run she won the bronze and brought home the second medal ever in the woman's marathon. She admitted she never strived to be the best, but to be the best she could be. Obviously she knew her best was not 4th place, which had become a fixed pattern in so many Olympics. Deena refused to quit until she reached her optimum potential, or optimistic potential.

Paula Radcliff, the top choice female marathon runner from Great Britain, is a perfect example of how we may defeat ourselves when the pressure is on hot and heavy. Paula was everyone's darling, including CNN who did extensive interviews with Paula regarding her life and anticipated victory. As expected by all, Paula was the leader of the pack right from the start of the race. When only 4 miles short of her victory, Paula fell into 6th place and quit. When the first person passed her she sensed defeat. Stricken with fear which creates pessimism, it seemed her spirit became completely deflated and she simply found no alternative to her emotional pain but to quit. We all felt her pain which was a result of a dehydrated belief system when her optimism was challenged. While the human body is built to run approximately twenty miles, it is optimism that allows us to overcome the deficiencies of the body and finish the final six. Optimism provides the hope that fuels the body to go the extra mile. Optimism is the little difference that makes the big difference.

Optimists tend to turn stumbling blocks into stepping stones that reflect the creative resourcefulness of winners. Adaptability is crucial in the survival of the fittest: not just in nature but in all our endeavors to excel. As you may know, the Chinese symbols for crisis are identical to those for the word opportunity. If we view adversity as corrective feedback, we do not feel defeated but enlightened. A poem by Gail Brook Burket reflects the attitude and mindset of winners:

I do not ask to walk smooth paths
Nor bear an easy load,
Pray for strength and fortitude
To climb the rock-strewn road.

Give me such courage I can scale
The hardest peaks alone,
And transform every stumbling block
Into a stepping-stone

Most people take the path of least resistance and as Peter Bentley said, "Most people are dancing on peanut butter," with most of their energy directed into defense, excuses, and justification of their treadmill life, rather than taking the risk and moving forward. Colleen Rubick, the woman runner from South Africa who at age 40 broke records by finishing the race in 2 hours, 46 minutes, and 35 seconds, stated her philosophy. "You can take two routes. One gets you home earlier, but I take the other or tougher route." Clearly there are no shortcuts to success.

Stand Like a Rock – Move Like a River

Taking no shortcuts, Matty Mathison is the recipient of the Disney Teacher of the Year Award and also the winner of the Herb Kohl Award for outstanding teacher. Matty climbed the Grand Teton in Jackson Hole, Wyoming, and completed fifteen consecutive American Birkebeiners, the largest cross-country ski race in North America.

Matty draws her inner strength from her deep connection with nature and her environment. She highly recommends creating a space of peace and tranquility whether you find it in New York City, by the beach, or in the woods. Matty referred to a Native American word, *mitakuye-oyasin*, which means "we are all related." Mattie lives in a log cabin that she heats with the wood that she cuts. She loves cold cheeks, frost on her eyelashes, and 28 degrees is her ideal climate—something

Wisconsin can provide in abundance. Not eccentric, Matty simply marches to her own drummer and thus loves the climbing wall in her living room with her flea market furniture as opposed to the refined Ethan Allen vintage.

Even in her fifties, Matty doesn't slow down, not even for fast running deer. While training on her roller blades at a leisurely 30 mph, a deer decided to cross her path and you can guess who won. However the climb soon became all up hill. With severe back pain, the loss of her beloved dog, the suicide of their high school principal, along with the move to a new school, Matty fell into the "dark night of the soul." The only escape from her depression seemed to be a suicidal plan where she would drop from a rock-climbing excursion so her death would appear accidental. While the support of others certainly helped, Matty drew strength from a belief in those magical words that gently whispered in her ear, "You can do it." The strength is in all of us, but we have to take the time to listen and tune into it. It was later that same year that Matty rose from the depths of despair and received the Disney Teacher of the Year Award. Even when the hills are high, we must keep climbing.

Although a competitive volleyball coach whose teams went to five Wisconsin State Championships, Matty benched a player because she was degrading her teammates which cost the team the conference championship. Winning isn't everything, integrity is. It's *how* you play the game that sets you apart.

Matty's definition of winning is an internal struggle to improve and success is continuing that struggle, persevering, and eventually taking home the gold. Everything takes longer than we anticipate, so take the time to develop a winning attitude, which is not cheating or winning on steroids. There are no short cuts. Trash talk or show boat stuff is putting on a performance. She reminds her players that they are on a playing court, not a stage. How do you play the game?

Instant Inspiration: You Can Do It!

Knowing there is humility in winning, Matty recalled the pressure in the 1988 State Championship since they had taken second the previous year and had to do better. They *had* to take first. With a 41-0 winning season, the team's anxiety was stifling performance and interrupting "flow," as they lost round I and were 0-13 in round II when a decision had to be made. Do we give those eager spirits on the bench their one moment in time since scoring *a* point seemed an impossibility, or do we go for the gold in spite of defeat seeming inevitable?

In their final timeout, Matty assured her team that they still were superstars and that she was proud of them once again taking second. However, at that moment, a soft voice from a reserved player quietly whispered, "We are going to win this game." It was instant inspiration as the girls marched in quiet confidence onto a most intimidating environment, ready to teach a course in miracles. After a net serve from the opponent, a much needed ray of hope, the superstars went on to score fifteen consecutive points and win round II which made them virtually unstoppable and of course took the third game by no surprise with a score of 15-3. They went on to take the title of Wisconsin State Women's Volleyball Champions – 1988. Bash on regardless.

Everything happens for a reason to give logic, balance, and purpose and why it is happening is our opportunity to learn the lesson. Everything is relative, says Matty, whose brother-in-law, a quadriplegic, is happier than birds on a spring day when he wakes up without bedsores. Matty states that one of the worst things we can do in to continually compare ourselves to others because when we do we always come up second and then begin to identify with that losing station in life.

Dream Modification and Redirection

Losing a game does not make you a loser. Don't equate who you are with what you do, for it will compel you to do more and be very busy going nowhere rather than discovering your true self. Being alone with your own thoughts can be one of life's greatest challenges because we are dependent on doing rather than just being. The Indonesian word, *kukaro*, which means to "be" rather than to do, best describes the essence of self-discovery. Winning is being authentic and true to yourself. It is standing like a rock while moving like a river.

She cautioned against all-or-nothing thinking. We need to compromise as we develop limitations that the aging process can impose upon us. Our challenges may change to perhaps simply getting out of bed in the morning, which may require dream modification and a redirection of our goals. Our perception of joy in life is all relative to where we are. "I grumbled because I had to get up so early in the morning—until one morning I couldn't get up."

We are all products of many different influences in our lives. However, we all have the ability to re-create ourselves and shape our futures through the choices that we make to become more thoughtful, informed, articulate, insightful, and creative. Great thinkers first create the solution and then seek the problem they might solve. We are what we think and with our collective thoughts we create our world.

It is clear that while some people simply ride in the wagon, others choose to be pulling the wagon even when the load gets heavy. Winners do not let obstacles on their path get in the way of their destiny. Mozart composed three major works in six weeks during which time his mother died and his wife and daughter were both very ill. That's focus.

The 80/20 Rule: 80% Coast - 20% Make It Happen

Perhaps the 80/20 Rule applies to all of life. I am guessing that 80% of the population coasts on what the other 20% makes happen. For example, while some employees of US Airways called in sick as an unofficial strike, which put incredible hardship on a struggling airline, other employees worked overtime without pay to keep the company afloat. While billions of dollars are being sent to Indonesia, Sri Lanka, Thailand, and other Asian countries devastated by the recent tsunami, others will exploit the disaster and prey on the miseries of their own people. We saw the same outpouring of compassion, support, and assistance after 9/11 and hurricanes here in the United States, but unfortunately for the self-serving soul, despair and disaster is an opportunity to exploit for a few who are imprisoned by their own greed.

It's all about getting an ROI. Just as our return on financial investments is contingent upon how and where we place it, so too our successes are contingent upon how and where we invest and direct our focus of thoughts and energy. Optimism requires letting go of that which we cannot control to free up more of our energies and move forward on that which we can control to make it happen.

Optimists Know No Risks — They Just Take Them

The ultimate optimist who never coasts and continually makes things happen is my mother, Mildred (Millie) Kirchman Rabas. She is living proof that optimism increases health and longevity. At age 92 she still does her daily power walk of almost three miles. At 90 Millie finally retired from driving 5-ton trucks around the country. However, she has not retired, but merely redirected. The modeling career she began at 80 continues and has given her recent opportunities to ride elephants and tangle with Green Bay Packer players.

Due to a fall, Millie has recently quit bowling on a team with an average age of 28. She still boasts of her 212 game that she bowled at age 88. She continues to click her happy heels dancing polkas every Sunday afternoon, and dancing the polka makes aerobics feel like a relaxation exercise.

Winners are optimists who know no risks — they just take them! My mother and father, James Rabas, Sr. (Big Jim), bought a hotel in 1936, and one year later started a car dealership, Algoma Motors. They took a weekend off to celebrate their wedding. A few years later they bought a farm and on that property built a new store for their dealership in 1947 and a new home in 1948.

Although her father and other relatives were concerned about their "let's roll" attitude, there was never an ounce of fear or doubt for they simply knew they would make it, admitting that both of them worked sixteen-hour days for many years. Millie says, "You just do what you have to do." For her it was selling cars (she was the first saleswoman licensed in Wisconsin in 1939 when many women weren't even driving cars). While breaking sales records she also ran the hotel where she fed seventy fishermen three meals each day along with all the housekeeping. Oh yes, and then there were four of us children she reared quite well, I think. Throughout her busy schedule, I never once heard her complain nor have any of us ever heard her utter one negative word ever in 92 years.

My father passed on in 1989. Although he had no more than a grade school education, he was an intuitive mechanical and engineering genius according to many with a Ph.D. in mechanical engineering who are still trying to figure out some of his inventions. An entrepreneur extraordinaire, when Jim was just a teen he purchased a steam engine and grain combine to create his first business providing harvesting services to farmers. An uncommon, common man, "Big Jim" was featured on People, Places, and Things, a CBS special that interviewed interesting and outstanding people of the year.

Upon asking Millie what was in their DNA that brought two kids off the farm to rise above mediocrity she simply replied, "I can't explain it." However, she did admit that in addition to a lot of hard work, they both had an eye for opportunity and a future view of patterns, trends, and where the puck might go. Millie and Jim are a great example of the power of partnership not only in business, but as they graced the dance floor and in life. Their legacy lives on as Algoma Motors continues to grow and prosper under the leadership of my brothers Jim and Jeff Rabas.

The Optimist Creed
Promise Yourself-

To be so strong that nothing can disturb your peace of mind.

To talk health, happiness and prosperity to every person you meet.

To make all your friends feel that there is something in them.

To look at the sunny side of everything and make your optimism come true.

To think only of the best, to work only for the best, and to expect only the best.

To be just as enthusiastic about the success of others as you are about your own.

To forget the mistakes of the past and press on to the greater achievements of the future.

To wear a cheerful countenance at all times and give every living creature you meet a smile.

To give so much time to the improvement of yourself that you have no time to criticize others.

To be too large for worry, too noble for anger, too strong for fear, and too happy to permit the presence of trouble.

CHAPTER FIVE

PERCEPTIONS:
FROM PROBLEM SOLVING TO POSSIBILITIES

"We don't see things as they are.
We see things as we are."
Anais Nin

A new world is a new mind. Deep change can only come from within. Failures can be instructive. Logic alone is a poor prophet, for intuition is necessary to complete the picture. Revolutions are not linear, nor do they proceed but rather crystallize. They shift suddenly like patterns in a kaleidoscope. To the blind, all things are sudden. Our crises are not a breakdown, but rather a breakthrough. Drawing from our inner resources we can achieve a new dimension of mind where we can see more by seeing through the eye and not with it. The enemy of whole vision is our reasoning power's divorce from imagination, closing itself in steel. The left-brain logical mind has forever been making laws and moral judgments, which have smothered spontaneity, feeling, and art. The right brain is transcendent logic that is too fast and too complex to comprehend with everyday consciousness and its step-by-step reasoning.

We Both Fear and Crave Becoming Truly Ourselves

Our institutions violate nature, for education has failed to value art, feelings, and intuition. Language molds thought, and we confuse it with reality. Words can isolate things that can only exist in continuity. Thus we must acknowledge the limits of language. Through a positive rebellion and creative protest we can challenge the de-humanizing, depersonalizing process that induces the anesthesia that demands violence to feel anything at all.

Winners are those who serve the needs of life and show the world the strength and joy of people who have deep convictions without being fanatical; who are loving without being sentimental; imaginative without being unrealistic; and disciplined without submission. Denial is not an alternative to submission. We are given two essential strategies for coping: the way of avoidance or the way of attention. Champions know that suffering only hurts when we flee it and complain about it, or fear it and thus choose to go through it. The pain is the aversion. The healing magic is attention. Psychologist Abraham Maslow said, "Knowledge carries responsibility. Fear of knowing is very deeply a fear of doing." We both fear and crave becoming truly ourselves.

By shaking up old understandings and priorities, we perceive things with a new vision. Through exploration we release the inner knowing and then integrate the mysteries that unfold as we trust our inner guru and discover a new self in an old culture. We are captives of our idea of time, and we cannot leave the trap until we know we are in it. We are not liberated until we liberate and love others without emotional mortgages. As we accept the fact that the map is not the territory we experience non-linear understanding as "tuning in" rather than traveling from point to point and thus acknowledge natural completion times rather than rigid deadlines. We process information in parallel channels at the same time and thus we cannot be swept away by a symphony while analyzing the composition.

Science is only now verifying what humankind has known intuitively since the dawn of history. If the brain were so simple we could understand it, we would be so simple we couldn't. A winner's perception of the world is not that of an automaton, but rather as a work of art. The brain is more like a great thought rather than a great machine, for the act of objectifying alters what we hope to see and what we are looking for is what is looking. Events are effects of what we imagine or visualize, for an image held in a transcendental state may be made real. It may not be the brain that produces consciousness but rather consciousness that creates the appearance of the brain. It is still a wonder how ancient mystics "knew" before there were tools to understand.

When Success Becomes Our Focus We Lose It

Author of *The Platinum Rule* and CEO of Online Assessments, Dr. Tony Alessandra's first experience in problem solving was somewhat unconventional. While living in the projects of Brooklyn, he was told by his father that he would give young Tony the belt if he did not go back out and fight the kid who beat him up. Tony considered this a defining moment or life-changing experience that gave him the confidence which he channeled well and took himself from being a street fighter in New York City to a university professor and extremely successful speaker, author, and businessman. Tony also learned that it was not only how he perceived possibilities, but also how other people perceived him and thus provided possibilities. He mentioned that people were intimidated by how he carries himself and the confidence his body language exudes—all survival skills from growing up in an environment that respected the tough guys who won the fights. His street smarts probably have contributed more to his success than his Ph.D. He fondly recalls getting hooked on the winning experience, not just in street fights but also winning all the contests in his Catholic grade school where he sold the most Bibles and greeting cards. Tony has always been motivated by winning, or perhaps it's not losing. (He remembers his father's warning that if he did not get a degree his share of the inheritance would go to charity.)

Because people like Tony rise from the projects to Ph.D., Dr. Peter Farmer, a two-time Olympian from Australia, feels being a champion is instinctual and that either you are born with the spark or it doesn't light. Hammer throwing seduced him because of the challenge of solving problems and always being a bit better. He cautioned, however, that in life as in sports, when success becomes our focus…we lose it.

Desire Fuels Creativity

Jan DeLory, President of the Boston Professional Group, also learned survival skills at a young age. She attributes her growing pains and struggles as key factors to her business savvy and success. Jan had lost her mother at age 9, leaving her alone with an alcoholic father who soon remarried and brought Jan into a chaotic household with ten other children. She politely referred to it as an adversarial environment with no soccer mom in sight. When she reported that she was asked to help her stepsister with cocaine and heroin injections and had life-threatening fistfights, I recognized adversarial was not an exaggeration.

The children shared underwear and nowadays many children don't even share a bathroom! Her alcoholic father had bailed out after the first year, leaving Jan in this totally dysfunctional mess to fend for herself with no support from anyone.

After years of pleading, her father rescued her when she was 15 years old and brought Jan to his one bedroom apartment where the kitchen became her bedroom. She had no clothes so a closet was not necessary. (What teenage girl needs a closet anyway.) Jan was her sole support and thus needed to work to survive.

If we have to lie or die, most of us would compromise our values. To eat Jan had lied and said she was her older sister and thus got a job at age 13 at Friendly's Ice Cream. She got paid a few coins and all the ice cream she could eat. She promoted herself very quickly and went on to bigger and better pastures and at age 14 worked for an answering service with headsets, cords, and all the trimmings. She was learning phone etiquette at an age when most children don't even grunt "hello" when they answer the family phone. By age 16 Jan was on her way to being a sales superstar, now selling automotive parts and motor oil to car dealers. Jan multi-tasks quite well and completed her first year of college at Northeastern University while finishing her senior year in high school. However, her not so enlightened father who always competed with Jan and resented her successes said, "Why do you want to go to college because you'll just get pregnant and married anyhow." I did clarify with Jan that his prediction was in that order...pregnant and then married.

As self-fulfilling prophecy would have it, Jan followed her father's prediction and got pregnant at age 19 to the stock boy at a grocery store where she was the office manager. (Now that's marrying up!) He prohibited her from working and thus she found herself living on the streets with her baby. In fact, they broke into the old apartment from which they had been evicted to at least have a roof over their heads. That was a moment of truth…and change.

Competition Puts Fire in the Belly

To feed her baby she took a job at *The Boston Globe* where her entrepreneurial spirit paid off. With commissions and bonuses she was rewarded not for time but for performance and as a part-time employee made more than any of the full-time staff. I want to also note that Jan commuted four hours by bus each day to work but four hours. If you can't, you must…if you must, you can. Desire fuels creativity. The painter, Michelangelo, confirmed the power of desire. "Lord, grant that I may always desire more than I can accomplish."

Although her colleagues thought she had lost it, her productivity came from having a phone in each ear. God gave us two ears, so why would you waste one of them. Then a college kid who had been hired tried three phones and the competition put a fire in her belly to rise above a boring job and continually improve her achievement level.

Jan's best friend's father, regarded as "a character," then hired Jan to manage the inside sales department, where she learned much from her new boss about leadership. He never lost his cool, stayed calm, was a problem solver, invested in his people, and created a fun environment. He had no MBA or any other degrees, but he did have an intuitive sense that was applied well in influencing others. (Shall we call it *schmooze*?)

As most champions, Jan learned to roll the dice and at age 23 as a single parent, Jan started her own remodeling company that did not do well, and the doors were closed after eighteen months. (Notice Jan did not say that it failed.) Continuing in sales, Jan then moved to Nashville where she sold pools during the day and wrote music lyrics at night. When her apartment burned to the ground and everything was lost, including her daughter's favorite doll, she moved back to Boston.

Circumstances Can't Crush Dreams

Receiving no child support, her survival skills kicked in once again. Not having a car and walking in heels for miles and miles until her feet were literally bleeding, Jan created a new position for herself where a car was provided. Having mastered survival, Jan then took a very lucrative job and immediately was in the top ten of 120 representatives, but the CEO decided to cut the top 25 sales representatives because of high compensation. What a brilliant move. You fire your top team bringing in all the sales so you don't have to pay the higher commissions. Could this be perverted reverse psychology?

To connect all the dots Jan engaged a life coach who helped her transform her dream into reality, and she began her own sales consulting group three years ago. Owning your own business is like being on 100% commission. It has high rewards for those who go the extra mile. Living on the edge triggers her competitive spirit and forces her to stretch her boundaries of which there seem to be none.

Here's the secret. Your environment may create an unhealthy reality but it can never steal your dreams. Her father tried, her husband attempted it, as did her unseasoned boss, but as Eleanor Roosevelt claimed, "No one can make you feel inferior without your consent." We all have control of our inner world and create our own realities from our hidden secrets and aspirations. In the Nazi concentration camps the Jews were stolen of dignity and choice. Carved into the walls of the camps were butterflies, a symbol providing a sense of hope by their freedom through flight.

Jan feels she was born with a good dose of drive and that as a little girl she always had huge dreams of being an actor, writer, or something bigger than life. She also reminded me that for the first nine years of her life she was blessed with a very supportive, loving mother who had become a Jehovah Witness and taught her strong spiritual laws. The irony is that after her mother's passing on she went into a household where they celebrated Christmas with a tree stolen from the neighbor's florist shop. Jan is living proof of the importance of early influences and learned values.

Illusions and the Demons of the Mind

In the movie, *Wall Street*, a rookie stock broker asked his mentor, played by Michael Douglas, "When is enough…enough? How many boats can you water-ski behind?" Many people who are unaware of the spiritual limitations of having only financial success turn to drugs, alcohol, sexual exploits, and gambling in an attempt to numb themselves of the pain and boredom of a meaningless and empty existence. When their genuine attempts to heal themselves fail, they seek even more of the same stimulation that creates an even greater void inside that we clinically call depression. We have seen it in many celebrities who have unfortunately found suicide as the only answer or solution to a problem which left them feeling so powerless, hopeless, and despairing in spite of their financial wealth and perceived power.

Obviously their self-concept and inner image did not match up to the perceived image of their fans who need to create idols because of their own emptiness and lack of identity. They thus project onto their heroes all that they wish and aspire to be, but have not developed the discipline and focus to live their own dreams and thus live vicariously through their favorite rock star or football hero. The expectations of cognitive dissonance, the lack of authenticity caused by the inconsistency between our inner image and our perceived value by the outside world, leaves us feeling even less deserving of the false nature of our stature. To resolve the conflict we then initiate a series of destructive self-sabotaging and self-defeating behaviors to destroy the illusions of Godliness and thus create an outside reality consistent with the demons in our mind.

It Is Our Light Not Our Darkness That Frightens Us

Millions of people each year are lured into one diet after another, even though the statistics indicate that eighty-five to ninety-five percent of all diets fail. As a psychotherapist I find hypnosis a very efficient and powerful tool to help people change their behavior. The reason for its effectiveness, now validated by research, is that it helps people change their thinking from the inside, or "insight" out. It creates new images, new beliefs and thinking patterns on the nonconscious level which is the powerhouse of our being. The nonconscious represents five sixths of our brain that most people never even tap into and explains the discouraging reports on the small percent of our potential that is ever actualized as confirmed by Oliver Wendell Holmes. "What lies behind us and what lies before us are tiny matters compared to what lies within us."

Without integrating the nonconscious mind we are trying to accomplish a job with just one horse when another five are available and ready to run the race. It is like digging a ditch with a spoon when a shovel or even a bulldozer is at our disposal. God certainly was not pleased with the steward who, with all good intentions, buried his talents. Yet most people fear to unleash their own potential for greatness. What is your fear? What is your potential for greatness and what are you waiting for? "Our deepest fear is not that we are inadequate. Our deepest fear is that we are powerful beyond measure. It is our light, not our darkness, that most frightens us," as explained by the author Marianne Williamson.

We all hear the phrase, "change your mind...change your life," but it is our choice to make that happen. We must learn how the mind works and then acquire the tools and systems for change to then move forward in accomplishing our desired goals.

If You Can't Stand Up – Stand Out!

Some obstacles are impossible to remove to reach our ideal goals and thus the only thing we can change is our attitude. Mike Schlappi, a two-time Paralympic Gold Medal winner and author of *Bulletproof Principles for Personal Success,* had a promising future in sports shattered when his friend accidentally shot him, leaving him paralyzed at age 14. Turning crisis into caring and sharing, Mike now inspires others with his recipe for success, "Attitude Therapy," which is a therapy we give to ourselves as we seek to recover from the inside out. It is learning to sculpt, change, or reframe the way we think. Mike cited Dallin H. Oaks, a noted Supreme Court judge who listed the three ingredients that comprise the inner man (or woman):

1. Motives—which explain actions completed
2. Desires—which identify actions contemplated.
3. Attitudes—which are the thought processes by which we evaluate our actions and experiences.

Mike emphasized that we sow seeds of constructive habits and internalize habits of self-progress, rather than those of self-destruction. Mike summed up the core challenge for attitude therapy with an insightful excerpt from Portia Nelson's *Autobiography in Five Short Chapters*:

Chapter I
I walk down the street.
There is a deep hole in the sidewalk.
I fall in.
I am lost...I am helpless.
It isn't my fault.
It takes me forever to find a way out.

Chapter II
I walk down the same street.
There is a deep hole in the sidewalk.
I pretend I don't see it.
I fall in again.
I can't believe I am in the same place.
It isn't my fault.
It still takes a long time to get out.

Chapter III
I walk down the same street.
There is a deep hole in the sidewalk.
I see it is there.
I still fall in - it is a habit.
My eyes are open.
I know where I am.
It is my fault.
I get out immediately.

Chapter IV
I walk down the same street.
There is a deep hole in the sidewalk.
I walk around it.

Chapter V
I walk down another street.

Mike's motto: *If we resist change, we'll fail; if we accept change, we'll survive; and if we create change, we'll succeed.* His keys to freedom are the following bulletproof principles:

1. Live to grow and to change, rather than to merely exist. Tackle life with a passion.
2. Learn to take responsibility for your attitudes and your actions rather than project blame or allow seeds of anger be in control of your emotional response.
3. Live not only to accept adversity but also to relish the acceptance of it. After all, the finest steel is made in the hottest furnaces, and thus Mike calls this strategy "refiner's fire."
4. Live with a "Service Mentality," by contributing to society rather than scavenging.
5. Live for a family rather than just with one.
6. Learn to laugh.

Mike has learned that if you can't stand up...stand out! Drew Becker, CEO of Convey Ink, also warns against self-centric behaviors and cited thoughts by Brendan Francis. "If you have a talent, use it in every which way possible. Don't hoard it. Don't dole it out like a miser. Spend it lavishly like a millionaire intent on going broke."

Not What If or Why Me, But What Is

In a very different challenge but perhaps a similar attitude, the author of *Race You to The Top*, Tony Christiansen, survived his double amputee caused by his legs being crushed by a train running over them when he was just 9 years old. In spite of his minor setback of having no legs, Tony has a black belt in Tae Kwon Do, is a qualified lifeguard, a speedway and racecar champion as well as a loving husband and father of three. Tony simply states that life is way too short and there simply is no time to get caught up in the "what if" or "why me" thoughts. Instead, Tony prefers "what is" which propels a forward focus. Making the most of his misfortune, Tony has accomplished so much more than most people with all their limbs even dream of doing. Tony admits he simply loves to win and that even if he places second or third in a race, he still is yahooing, yelling, and screaming, for it is the joy of competing that gets his motors running. Do you know what gets your motors running and what excuses are getting in the way of your personal victory of living the life you most desire?

Obviously nothing gets in the way for Mattie Stepanek, a young boy whose poetry, which he has been writing since age 3, explores the uncensored reality of living with a rare form of muscular dystrophy as well as the grief of losing three siblings to the same life-threatening condition. How is that for an optimistic attitude? Most kids can't cope with a scratched CD! Knowing it's how you look at it, Mattie not only tolerates and accepts but embraces his disease to increase his understanding of his life experience with physical limitations. Mattie celebrates each day as a gift—with humor and a boy's passion for fun. You may have seen Mattie on Oprah, Good Morning America, or Larry King Live. His list of awards, including that of National Goodwill Ambassador, is too lengthy to mention, but he definitely echoes the wisdom, compassion, and consciousness of Gandhi.

Dream Up: Dwell in Possibility

In my interview with W. Mitchell, a speaker, author, and TV host, he presented his mantra with strong conviction. "Its not what happens to you, it's what you do with what happens." W. Mitchell had overcome two life-changing accidents—the first a fiery motorcycle accident and the second an airplane crash. He strongly emphasizes that while we don't always have control over what happens to us, we do have a choice regarding how we respond and deal with what happens, which is our point of power. We truly do create the world we choose, one choice at a time. The following best describes W. Mitchell's attitude, strength, and joy. "Before I was paralyzed there were 10,000 things I could do. Now there are 9.000. I can either dwell on the 1,000 I've lost or focus on the 9,000 I have left."

People who embrace possibility thinking are capable of accomplishing the impossible because they believe in solutions. Then too, the MindShift of possibility thinking activates the laws of attraction that bring more possibilities into your sphere of influence. Because it is contagious, people who think "big picture" attract big people who then create big possibilities for others. It is a reciprocal, symbiotic, synergistic process that swells as you dwell...in possibilities.

If you are not ready to take the big leap forward into your future, at least let go of the mental crutches and ankle weights. Bob Rotella, a sports psychologist, allows some concessions. "I tell people: If you don't want to get into positive thinking, that's OK. Just eliminate all the negative thoughts from your mind, and whatever's left will be fine." If you are of the belief that optimistic, possibility thinkers and dreamers are unrealistic and naïve, then read the previous chapters again and again, until you get it. An alternative would be to list as many negative, cynical, impossibility thinkers you know who have accomplished great things.

Refuse the status quo and cultivate a possibility mind-set by continually dreaming just a bit bigger. Henry Curtis suggests, "Make your plans as fantastic as you like, because twenty-five years from now, they will seem mediocre. Make your plans ten times as great as you first planned, and twenty-five years from now you will wonder why you did not make them fifty times greater. If you believe you can't do something, no matter how hard you try, you have already lost. The perception of problems as possibilities is a way of 'seeing' that can be developed with the direction of purpose, the power of passion, and the determination of desire."

No Rules for Success Will Work Unless You Do

Somers White, executive coach and business consultant supreme, is an icon of the determination of desire. He states that a lot of success is basic self-discipline, which is doing what you really don't want to do when you know it needs to be done. Somers has a lot of both right and left-brain talents. He has broad vision but also pays attention to details, proving classmates wrong when they voted him the least likely to succeed. Even with dyslexia, Somers was reading on a sixth grade level in first grade and graduated from the Harvard Business School. After eighteen months with Chase Bank on Wall Street, he became the president of The Northwest Bank, and also became an Arizona state senator, and wrote *High Impact Living* and *High Impact Selling* in his spare time.

Success is self-sustaining for once you experience its sweetness you want more and begin to crave dessert. Somers emphasized that not only success leaves clues but so does potential disaster as we now see in the aftermath of 9/11. Nothing ever went bad without first going slow. He urged us all to be alert, aware, and observant of the spot of blood on the armor, for there are always early warning signs whether it may be to ward off an attack or prevent financial ruin. He also advised that we listen to our gut.

The Best Prospects Are the Rush of Good Ideas

Somers feels preparation and having the ability to anticipate and prepare for the storm have contributed to his success as well as going the extra mile, even in menial jobs which became monumental because of his enthusiasm, organization, and system thinking. I have attended Somers' large, lavish dinner parties where he admitted to easily saving about $15,000 by paying only for the empty bottles, which he marks with a stamp to manage and control operations. Preparation and perfection pay...or at least save. Even the Marriott was amazed at his system of accountability that pays great dividends. His attention to detail gives Somers three months off to travel each year in spite of speaking in fifty states and six continents.

Citing President Reagan's magic as a connector, Somers emphasized that winners understand the value of "connection" which is why he sends real letters instead of e-mail, which he considers a debased currency—quick and easy. He affirms the Internet as a media, but not as a business, stating that as we become disconnected in our online society, human contact becomes a more crucial factor in making a difference. When you are with someone be totally present rather than look for opportunity elsewhere with the wandering eye. Networking events often are a display of people defeating themselves by the invalidation of their vacant presence. While Somers felt champions are more often made, he also added that no one makes it alone and that the best prospects are the rush of new ideas.

A social worker turned capitalist, Somers fits no molds, but his success strategies are simple. "No rules for success will work unless you do." He emphasized early experiences of accomplishment and success to establish an anchor or reference point. It begins the success cycle: once we receive the recognition, we hunger for more, which gives us the drive and motivation to repeat it again and again to the point that we expect it, believe in ourselves, and know that we deserve it. His father and Jim Combs, a football coach who took nineteen championships, never accepted anything less than doing your very best. He added that without hope, we're dead in the water, for it is hope that is expecting a positive outcome that moves us in the direction of our dreams literally.

Being a strategic thinker, Somers' exit strategy is death, with an early retirement party planned for his funeral. "What doesn't grow… dies." Yet so many people insist on growing old. Anton Chekhov, the Russian playwright, obviously agrees with Somers in writing:

The joy of living is everywhere and available to all, but people have been blinded to it. It is there before them, but they do not know it. It is priceless, but they place no value on it. It is tempting but they are not tempted. It satisfies all longings, but they do not long. It offers youth, but they insist on growing old.

CHAPTER SIX

BORN TO WIN:
ARE CHAMPIONS MADE OR BORN?

"Why do some people who are born with so much, achieve so little, while some who are born with so little achieve so much? The answer is 'desire!' You must have a great desire."
Lou Holtz

Destiny is not a matter of chance; it is a matter of choice. Although some of those interviewed said champions were born, more affirmed that they were made. The majority, however, saw those who had lived their dreams as people who were more aware of their special gifts and in sync with their instincts. Either they themselves or someone else such as a parent, teacher, coach, friend, grandparent, or other family member recognized their strengths and innate abilities and nurtured them to fruition. The spark that ignited their passion gave direction to their purpose and the indomitable will that made them unstoppable.

Their desire dominated their fears and moved them in the direction of their destiny. In fact, they were so focused on their goals and dreams that there was a lack of awareness of any fears or consequences other than the fear of never singing their song. There was a pleasantly haunting voice from within that said, "Just do it," and they did. They knew what had to be done and they could not sleep until it was accomplished to the very best of their ability. Optimism was not an option but the core of an undying belief system that would allow them to bash on regardless.

I'm Just a Pencil in the Hand of God

Just as Abe Lincoln was immune to rejection and kept his face to the wind, so were Jack Canfield and Mark Victor Hansen when they relentlessly attempted to find a publisher who recognized the value of their book, *Chicken Soup for the Soul.* The series now has eighty-two editions and each year nine more are created.

Jack and Mark Victor Hansen, the coauthor, persisted after 144 publishers rejected the popular manuscript.   In two days they received over one hundred rejections and their agent, exhausted after twenty-two pitches, admitted she simply could not sell it.   Finally Health Communications saw the light, and as Paul Harvey would say, now you know the rest of the story.   In addition to the famous *Chicken Soup for the Soul* series, Jack has written other books including *The Power of Focus,* and his most recent release, *The Success Principles.*

Jack is living proof of the beliefs, theories, and stories presented by the many other champions interviewed. Here are a few of the common threads in the tapestry of success that Jack not only discussed but demonstrates in his daily living.

1. Authenticity—You must be consistent and first become who you are before you can do great things. Even Shakespeare recognized that personal truth when he said, "To thine ownself be true." Jack is real, authentic, and obviously walks his talk.

2. Mentoring: Hang Out with People of Greatness – Jack mentioned that a turning point in his life was in 1970-1972, during which time he worked with W. Clement Stone, a pioneer and author of success principles, and developed a true belief in himself and all that he might do.

3. Take Responsibility for Your Life—A second turning point was the influence of another coach and mentor, Robert Resnik, a Gestalt therapist.

4. Decide What You Want—Visualize your desires as if they have already manifested themselves in vivid details.

5. Power of Belief—Believe it is possible and believe in yourself.

6. Clarity of Vision and Focus—Another teacher was Martha Crampton who helped Jack become more integrated and centered to provide an inner peace.

7. The Purpose-Driven Life—In response to my question of what drives him, Jack admitted he had a vision of making a difference in the world before he was born. He knows he was born to teach people to create the life they want rather than the life they found themselves in. He has since officially created a mission or life purpose statement:

   To impact one billion lives. To inspire and empower people to live their highest vision in a context of love and joy.

   While I would not consider this to be a trivial task, it obviously has been or will be completed soon. This is the magic we create when we are clear why we are here. Jack's favorite quote by Mother Teresa well reflects his transcendence from success to significance being based on servantship. "I'm just a pencil in the hand of God."

8. Create a Plan—People don't plan to fail; they fail to plan.

9. Play the Game—Roll the dice, take informed risks, and take the actions necessary to make it happen.

10. Hang in There—Persist and persevere until you get what you want.

11. Clone Your Success—Create a system of success to leverage your time and talents so that you free up your time and energy to serve better and enjoy life more.

12. Partner for Prosperity—Magnify your talent and multiply your efforts by creating partnerships and teams.

Luck may also be a factor, but it is hard to determine what is luck and what is part of a divine plan. Jack admitted he was given special opportunities by a wealthy aunt who had lost her son, also named Jack. She thus made Jack Canfield a surrogate son and paid for his private education. Being from Wheeling, West Virginia, Jack may have had another lucky break as he was accepted into the prestigious Harvard University under a geographic distribution program that admitted at least two students from each state.

A True Player Discovers One's Truth and Authentic Self

Like Dr. Charles Petty, he turned his survival skills into assets. Jack's natural father was abusive. Thus Jack became, and still is, hyper-vigilant, a skill that allows him to size up a room in seconds which is not a handicap for a professional speaker. His parents divorced when Jack was 6 years old, and although his mother was an alcoholic with few aspirations, she loved people and instead of slamming the door on missionaries she would invite them in for dinner. His stepfather was a workaholic who had high expectations and did not tolerate giving up. I find it interesting when some people don't have good examples, they learn what not to do from the bad examples or extract some lesson from every experience.

Jack found himself and his greatness when he stopped hiding and responding from past conditioned behavior, such as being a people pleaser. We become a true player when we discover our truth and our authentic self. Jack cited the words of author J.D. Salinger to best describe his own personal transformation and growth. "One day a long time from now you'll cease to care anymore whom you please or what anybody has to say about you. That's when you'll finally produce the work you're capable of." It may be a bit of a vicious cycle as we often find the courage to stand up for ourselves only after we have produced our greatest work. We must affirm our psychological independence that in turn frees up our energies to focus and break through any barriers, imagined or real. He cited Daniel Amen's 18/40/60 Rule: When you're 18, you worry about what everybody is thinking of you; when your 40 you don't care what anyone thinks about you; when you're 60, you realize nobody's been thinking about you at all. (If they are thinking about you at all, they are wondering what you are thinking about them.) My suggestion is quit worrying about what other people think about you and follow your heart.

Tap Dance to Work

Warren Buffet, one of the richest and most successful businessmen in America, follows his heart all the way to the bank. When we are in sync with our instincts, everyday is a holiday and optimism comes easily. When asked to describe happiness, Warren answered, "Happy is what I am. I get to do what I like to do every single day of the year. I get to do it with people I like, and I don't have to associate with anybody who causes my stomach to churn. I tap dance to work and when I get there I think I'm supposed to lie on my back and paint the ceiling. It's tremendous fun…. I know I wouldn't be doing anything else. I'd advise you…to work for an organization of people you admire, because it will turn you on."

Coach Krzyzewski, better known as "Coach K" of the Duke University basketball team in Durham, North Carolina, turned down a lucrative offer of eight million from the LA Lakers to coach in the NBA. Coach K explained that he is where he wants to be, doing exactly what he wants to do, with people he respects and often loves. Winners are on a never-ending honeymoon. Unfortunately, we often numb ourselves from our awareness of what we want and who we are because we fear the repercussions of our need to act upon it.

We all have our gifts, and Thomas Quasthoff is elated with his. "If I could be normal and not sing, or sing and be disabled (which he is), I would sing." However, Tom had to connect the dots and roll the dice. Our focus needs to be less about the task at hand or our lofty goals and more so on ourselves and who we are: our gifts, strengths, talents, passion, and "calling" in life. It is developing a belief system within ourselves that gives us the courage to live our wildest dreams, which once we accomplish them, they aren't so wild at all…it is simply who we are.

Karen Stevens addresses being simply who we are and suggests that we become the person we were meant to be.

You can be all of the things you dream of being,
if you're willing to work at them and if you'll believe in yourself more.
You have a special understanding of people…
why they do the things they do; why they hurt; why they hurt others.
Learn from the mistakes of others…
accept them; forgive them.
Don't use the roles others have had in your life as excuses for your mistakes.
Take control, and live your own life.
Continue the journey you've begun: the journey inside yourself.
It is the most difficult journey you'll ever make, but the most rewarding.
Take strength from those you love, and let those who love you help.
Keep your pride, but don't live for it.
Believe in your own goodness, and then do good things. You are capable of them.

> *Work at being the person that you want to be.*
> *Sacrifice desires of the moment for long-term goals.*
> *The sacrifices will be for your benefit;*
> *you will be proud of yourself.*
> *As you approach life, be thankful for all the good things that you have.*
> *Be thankful for all the potential that you're blessed with.*
> *Believe in that potential – and use it.*
> *You are a wonderful person; do wonderful things.*
> *True happiness must come from within you.*
> *You will find it by letting your conscience guide you – listen to it; follow it.*
> *It is the key to your happiness.*
> *Don't strive to impress others, but strive to impress yourself.*
> *Be the person you were meant to be.*
> *Everything else will follow; your dreams will come true.*

We are all unique individuals with our own desires and expressions. Each of us has available our own inner guidance and our own knowledge of what is right for us. Follow your heart and happiness is yours.

If You're Not Working Out of Balance…
Your Checkbook Will Be

Author of The Wall Street Journal bestseller, *The Little Red Book of Selling* and *The Sales Bible*, Jeffrey Gitomer has found happiness by following his heart. A syndicated business columnist, Jeffrey claims that your gifts are your qualifiers. We are born with a set of skills, but it is our privilege and responsibility to discover and develop them—which well answers whether champions are made or born. In discussing drive and desire vs. the "just being" state of peace in the Buddhist doctrine, Jeff said that while he is very content with what he does, he is never satisfied until he has won, which of course with every victory comes a new challenge. His competition is only with himself, as winning for him is just doing a bit better each time around.

Regarding goals, Jeffrey has plenty, but money is not one of them, only those of improved achievement. (Just between you and me, Jeffrey doesn't need donations.) Although Jeffrey described himself as a selfish person in that he wants to be a better person, father, speaker, and husband for himself, others obviously benefit from what he refers to as selfish efforts. Such are the laws of reciprocity, and thus as we continually improve ourselves with integrity, everyone wins, for we are all so very much connected.

Jeffrey describes himself as informational and inspirational rather than motivational, which he sees as short-lived and must be an inside job. Like John DiLemme, he emphasizes that knowing your "why" is a primary driving force for achievement because it creates awareness and stirs emotion.

Winners Are Stimulated by Their Losses

Jeffrey's dad said you can't succeed unless you've failed a few times. I recall the University of Michigan doing a program on Entrepreneurship 101 and to teach the class you did not have to have a doctorate or even a bachelors degree, but you did have to have numerous bankruptcies or major setbacks. The setbacks are essential not only for their learning experiences: only risk takers who roll the dice are true entrepreneurs. Ask Donald Trump.

Jeffrey feels vacations are for people who hate what they are doing and feels his work is one on-going vacation. He admitted he is having a blast. "If you're not working out of balance, your checkbook will be." Learning from the successes and failures of his father who manufactured kitchen cabinets, Jeffrey feels that losing boosts one's business immunity by keeping you tuned up and more determined to win again. That theory does not work for everyone, as some people cry "uncle" in defeat. Actually that is a distinguishing factor between winners and those who come in second. Winners seem to be stimulated by their losses and get back in the ring faster and fight harder in the second round rejoicing in the opportunity. "The world is moving so fast these days that the man who says it can't be done is generally interrupted by someone doing it," according to the writer Elbert Hubbard.

To Be a Big Leaguer – Think Big League

Jeffrey recommends that if you want to succeed in sales and you did not grow up in the Northeast where only the tough survive, you need to go to New York City and cold call for a week, preferably in the garment district where before you make the appointment you hear, "Where's my bribe." Jeffrey proudly announced no bribe was ever given, as it's not how he plays the game.

In sales and in life a positive attitude is crucial. Jeffrey confessed that although he has been broke, he has never been down because of a lesson he learned from Glenn W. Turner whose furniture was repossessed the third time he went broke. Although his wife was devastated, Glenn was relieved at the opportunity of no more payments. We then need to ask ourselves questions of what we can do differently and in a sense sharpen our problem-solving skills, but never lose the magic of thinking big. Jeffrey quoted Benny Bengough of the New York Yankees. "To be a big leaguer, think big league."

Regarding retirement, Jeffrey said, "*I am* retired. Being retired means you get to do what you want and I am!" He also cited Les Paul who at the age of 89, stricken with arthritis, still plays the guitar at the Meridian in New York City. Les invented the electric guitar that is played by ninety percent of all lead guitarists. People who work until the day they die do so because they are not working but rather playing.

Never Yield to the Apparent Might of the Enemy

Rob Waite, another big thinker who is the author of *The Lost Art of General Management,* stressed that we can never let someone else tell us what we can or cannot do. At age 21, just out of college and on his first job, Rob challenged himself to double his income every five years and at age 43 he has kept his personal promise. Challenging ourselves is another way of expanding our goals and our vision. When Churchill gave his famous speech reminding people to never, never, never, never, never give in, he preceded those frequently quoted words with a demand that you never yield to the apparent might of the enemy. If nothing else, a good reason not to quit is because if you do the jerk on the other side wins.

Rob recalled Margaret Thatcher stating that she knew she was in the presence of greatness when she shared a meal with President Ronald Reagan and Sir Winston Churchill. However, she did note that Churchill made everyone feel that he was the smartest person in the room, while President Reagan made you feel like you were the smartest person in the room. This may be why due respect was returned to the former president at his overwhelmingly attended funeral, even after being out of the public eye for over a decade.

Making Adversaries Your Advocates

Whether you voted for him or not, whether you agreed or disagreed with his policies, President Reagan seemed hard to dislike as a person. He had humble beginnings as the son of an alcoholic shoe salesman from Illinois. However, he was blessed with a multitude of gifts or had one exceptional gift that took him to the top in a variety of roles not only as governor of California and president of the United States, but as a successful actor in fifty films. Reagan's magic was that he was able to remain so connected to his adversaries and opponents in fierce debates where they were somewhat disempowered or captured by his compassion. Reagan would continually frustrate Congressman Tip O'Neil who would come out of confrontations with the president because of a severe clash in political beliefs, but then would admit that he loved the guy, fondly referred to as "Dutch."

In the 1984 election Reagan carried all but one state, burying his opponent Walter Mondale. A gentle giant, Reagan's smile, warmth, and sincere caring created a bond with the American people and his personal communication style made him a model leader. He was compassionate but did what needed to be done even if it meant firing those he loved and respected. Senator Elizabeth Dole recalled the loving way in which the president felt she was not the right person for the position she had held and wanted. After announcing his decision to Elizabeth who at that time was the head of the Department of Transportation, he then called her back as she began to leave the room and said, "Elizabeth, I am so sorry."

Even in adversity he was able to see the light side. After only two months in office, President Reagan was shot by a lone gunman, John Hinckley, and his comment to Nancy, the First Lady, was "Honey, I forgot to duck." To the surgeons about to operate on him, he said: "I hope you are Republicans."

Reagan was not an instant success, but very persistent. Reagan had tried to capture the Republican nomination as early as 1968 and did not actually win the race until 1989 at the age of 69, being the oldest man elected to office. He was referred to as the "Teflon" president whose mistakes never stuck to him. He managed to survive the soaring budget deficit and the icy freeze in the relations with the Soviet Union with his reputation intact.

He admitted that he had approved sending military supplies to Iran in a blatant contradiction of the stated policy and left office with a budget deficit larger than the combined total of all of his thirty-nine predecessors, which may have made him a figurehead more than a strong leader with a grasp for detail. He was, nevertheless, believed by many to be the best communicator the White House had ever had and, for a while, made America feel good about itself again. He was the essence of hope, which is the fuel to the fires of greatness in all of us. With his eight years of disasters and triumphs, Reagan's most impressive reflection of his optimism was when he announced to the world that he wrote an open letter to the American people. In it he said: "I have recently been told I am one of the millions of Americans who will be afflicted with Alzheimer's disease…I now begin a journey that will lead me into the sunset of my life." Now that's optimism!

Not only in politics and business, but life in general, we all need to practice a basic respect for the dignity of all human beings, in which case slavery and segregation would have never existed or even been considered. We must always give reverence to the fact that none of us are in isolation, but oh so intricately connected and thus must monitor what we give out as it all comes back to us ten-fold.

The Truly Creative Mind Must Create

Tom Quasthoff, one of the finest bass-baritones doing eighty concerts a year in Germany and around the world, truly connects with his audiences. Although blessed with an incredible voice, he was born with no arms which prevented him from singing on the stage he so dearly loved. Born in 1959 as a thalidomide baby, his parents had sent him to an institution but knew he was gifted with a singing intelligence. In spite of his deformed body, being a dwarf and having no arms, Thomas feels blessed and is living his dream. Initially his deformity caused him to be rejected for roles in his beloved operas and thus felt forced into law.

(Apparently judges and critics were a bit confused and somehow thought arms were a qualifier for singing.) As the world of music became enlightened, Thomas eventually played center stage and recalled the agony of being in law when he knew inside he was an artist and simply wanted to be who he was born to be.

The author Pearl S. Buck echoed the same refrain:

> *The truly creative mind in any field is no more than this: a human creature born abnormally, inhumanly sensitive. To him a touch is a blow, a sound is a noise, a misfortune is a tragedy, a joy is an ecstasy, a friend is a lover, a lover is a god, and failure is death. Add to this cruelly delicate organism the overpowering necessity to create, create, create — so that without the creating of music or poetry or books or buildings or something of meaning, his very breath is cut off from him. He must create, must pour out creation. By some strange, unknown, inward urgency he is not really alive unless he is creating.*

People are viciously loyal to their passion once they are clear on what it is. Thomas confessed that if he could be physically normal in exchange for his voice, "I would stay the way I am. My life is a film for which I don't know the end. I'm a very happy man." Now that he is in love, Tom is even happier.

The Loving Mirror

Having someone who loves us helps us see our value and our worth.
In my interview with the author of *Permission to Succeed,* Noah St. John explained his concept of the "loving mirror." He emphasizes that we don't see our own value and that it is through relationships that we acquire an awareness and appreciation of our own self-worth. An example Noah gives is asking people what color their eyes are. Although most answer with accuracy, he then asks how they know the color of their eyes. Noah has made his point. Everyone answers, "I looked in the mirror."

Noah gave convincing examples of the support received by Tiger Woods from his father; Les Brown from his teacher who refused to allow him to refer to himself as retarded; and the support Mary Todd Lincoln gave to her beloved husband and one of the most revered presidents, Abraham Lincoln. It was Mary Todd who saw the bigger picture for him, for Abe saw himself merely as a simple country lawyer. The history of the United States could be a different book had Mary Todd not believed in him even after losing election after election. That type of psychological resilience and bounce-back ability can rarely be sustained alone.   An example I often share is the story of Stevie Wonder, who took on the name "Wonder" thanks to his grade school teacher who referred to Stevie as such "a wonder."

Noah's suggestions for success flips upside down the traditional messages to succeed in that they often encourage us to believe in ourselves, which obviously is the end goal of all foundations to success. However, in America the spirit of rugged individualism may be omitting the most important factor in personal and professional success...relationships.   Actually I can still hear my mother's empowering words to both my sister and me. "Behind every great man...is a woman."   My mother is 92 years old, and back in those days it was often a woman's only claim to fame.

Always having been a student of the powers of mind, I was personally intrigued by a couple of Noah's concepts. While many of us have been repeating our positive affirmations and have been aware that the brain goes into an automatic retrieval of the answer when we ask the question, Noah has transformed affirmations into empowering *afformations*. Hopefully no one asks questions such as "Why am I such a loser?" Obviously this is not a constructive approach to positive change! I had to chuckle as Noah mentioned that his now current wife and soul mate saw his afformation on his desk that reads, "Why did she finally come to me and stay?" She confidently tore it down and said, "I believe this job is taken." For all of you still searching for your soul mate, you may want to try what worked so well for Noah. Just as Christ would thank in advance, we too must give thanks for that which we choose to attract into our lives.

There's No Fate but What We Make

Noah St John's response to whether people are born as champions was that we are not born, but reborn, with life being a continual rebirthing process. He commented that Tiger Woods, after winning The Masters at age 19 by twelve strokes, took a painful dive into a muddy sand trap.

Tiger spent over two years remaking his swing. He came back stronger than ever by taking the trophy in Spain and then winning all four majors in sequence which was a record not set since Bobbie Jones. Like Bonnie St. John said, it's not always how fast you ski, but if and how fast you bounce back when you hit the patches of ice in your life. Winners and champions demonstrate the patience, persistence, and perseverance to meet the challenge of continually being reborn. In fact, they embrace it! As said in *The Terminator*, "There's no fate but what we make."

Noah emphasized that we all need an idol, mentor, and coach to not only guide us and give us direction and vision but to supersede them. Tiger Woods topped his idol, Jack Nicklaus. Tom Brady of the Patriots idolized Joe Montana, but he also went above and beyond his role model. What an honor to have contributed to the rebirthing of another who has taken our seed and blossomed into full bloom. A book entitled *Invisible Loyalties* addresses the psychological barrier by which many are squelched in feeling that to respect their parents, they must not exceed the health and wealth of those before them. I remember when I was in Egypt, the tour guide mentioned that each pyramid following the one built for the previous king was a few centimeters less to show respect. While Tom and Tiger are not tearing down tombs, they are great guides to give you permission to succeed.

Noah certainly has been in a permanent state of being reborn, for he was previously a ballet dancer who retired at age 22 due to an injury. He then went to Los Angeles to do some acting and actually did do acting, not just wait on tables. Born again into an author at age 30 when just out of college, he is now getting his Ph.D. in psychology. I am old enough to remember that if you changed careers more than once or did not stay on the family farm or same factory that your great grandfather built, you were a bit unstable. Obviously society is also growing.

Destiny Is That Picture in Your Mind

As testimony to Noah's theory, Robert Zimmerman was reborn as Bob Dylan. The question that got the most mixed response in my interviews was, "Are champions made or born?" However in an interview conducted by Morley Safer with Bob Dylan aired on 60 Minutes (CBS) on December 5, 2004, Bob Dylan answered that question with much certainty. Bob Dylan grew up as Robert Zimmerman in the wide-open spaces of rural Minnesota to very traditional parents who thought the capitol of the world was wherever they lived. When Morley asked him if he had a happy childhood, Dylan stated that he did not know if it was happy or unhappy, which was not important. What was important was what he felt he needed to do. He remembers destiny looking at him and nobody else. He explained destiny as that picture in your mind that you just know will become a reality, but you learn to keep that vision to yourself or someone may kill it. He admitted to changing his name to Bob Dylan due to destiny and admitted that sometimes we are given the wrong name and perhaps the wrong parents.

Bob confessed that he always knew he would be a music legend and when he moved to Greenwich Village in New York City, he found his true home and came alive. By age 25 Bob had become a cultural and political icon, a voice of the time and that generation. I found it fascinating that Bob never saw himself as anything but a musician while his peers projected their needs for a protest leader upon him, which he feels was their illusion and not his reality. While Bob was simply writing and singing songs, the protest movement adopted them as anthems and sermons, anointing him as spokesman, prophet, and savior. Those more conventional saw Bob as a threat to society, when again he simply wished to just sing his songs. Throughout history the mobs and masses have always created idols to adore and worship, starting with the golden calf.

It can be frustrating to be so misunderstood and although attempts were made to destroy the false image created by a politically hungry crowd, Bob Dylan finally retreated to Woodstock, New York, where people followed him to discuss things they assumed their "all natural" guru would have expertise such as organic farming. I guess it would be like asking a friendly farmer how to compose a symphony. He so desperately sought to break the false, manufactured icon of who he was that he deliberately made bad records and even traveled to Israel and had himself filmed wearing a skull cap at the wailing wall after all other attempts such as wearing white makeup as a mask did not crack the code.

Bob had earned three Grammy Awards in 1988, did over one hundred concerts per year and at age 63 got a second spark and is on the road again. He has recently written his biography with promises of more to come and he was recently nominated for the Nobel Prize for his songs as a contribution to literature. When asked why he is where he is today in terms of achievements he simply responded, "The destiny thing. I'm just holding up my end of the bargain with the Chief Commander."

I Will Be Dead If I Don't Compose

That destiny thing is certainly true for others such as Mozart who was writing symphonies by age 3. A modern-day Mozart, Jay Greenberg was also born with a very special musical gift. According to the Juilliard School of Music in New York City, Jay Greenberg has already composed five symphonies, and may be the first person so gifted in a couple hundred years. Jay states complete musical compositions come fully written in his head and thus in just a couple hours he can complete a symphony and a sonata in twenty-five minutes.

His parents are 36 years old. His father is of Slavic descent and is blind, while his mother is a painter from Israel. They report that Jay was drawing and writing the word cello at age 2, along with drawing other instruments, and was composing by age 3. Jay can process multiple channels of input at the same time and process three different musical works at once.

Unlike Beethoven, who was never satisfied and was constantly crossing things out, young Greenberg does not revise or edit because it all comes to him right the first time. To avoid boredom, Jay will do mundane tasks such as taking Beethoven's Ninth Symphony and invert it and play it upside down and backwards. (Maybe Jay needs to challenge himself a bit with more TV viewing.) He writes what he cannot play and confesses that he must compose. "I will be dead if I don't compose," which qualifies him as having a purpose-driven life.

"If we look at the path,
We do not see the sky.
We are earth people
On a spiritual journey
to the stars.
Our quest, our earth walk
is to look within,
to know who we are,
to see that we are connected
to all things,
that there is no separation,
only in the mind."

Native American, source unknown

CHAPTER SEVEN

THE WINNING HABIT:
LEADERSHIP AND THE INDOMITABLE WILL

> *"Winning is not a sometime thing; it's an all the time thing.
> You don't win once in a while, you don't do things right once
> in a while, you do them right all the time. Winning is a habit.
> Unfortunately, so is losing."*
> ### Vince Lombardi

Ben Franklin, a disciplined man with winning habits, may have best described the invincible, indomitable will of champions. "I haven't failed. I've had 10,000 ideas that did not work." As Bonnie St. John said, "Olympians lose more than anyone else. If you're not willing to lose more and be bad at something, you'll never be good at it. The champion mindset is a willingness to lose; otherwise who would try." Remember it was Bonnie who skied faster but took silver at the Paralympics in Austria because when she fell on the same ice as her competition she did not get back up as quickly as the German skier who took the gold.

Feelings: A Printout of Your Thoughts

In our journey for the gold, the key factor may be how quickly we get back up. How can you shorten your recovery time from falls, setbacks, and bruises along the way? More than not enough money, time, or lost resources, I find the key factor to shortening the recovery cycle is, as Dr. Phil would say, "Deal with it." Whining, wishing, and playing the "what if" game causes us to lose valuable time and energy that could be redirected to move forward. The clock keeps ticking not only at the Olympics but in your own life as well.

Jill Lublin, author of *Guerilla Publicity* and *Networking Magic*, simply stops the clock with a concept she got from Jane Strauss, called "time in." It's when she totally disconnects from the world and does a personal audit. Through structure, setting boundaries, and saying "no," she has created more personal freedom and has stopped stealing from herself. In her "turtle time" she quietly puts her brain on *pause*. This has increased her creativity, productivity, and pleasure.

The greatest barrier to reaching your goals and achieving the gold is your *chosen* reaction to the 10,000 ideas that did not work. If you feel defeat, despair, fear, and take on a "loser" attitude and never try again, very simply you are defeated and the game is over. It is thus not only how you look at it, but how you look at yourself. Dr. Dennis Deaton of Quma Learning Systems emphasizes awareness, stating that we must think about what we are thinking in the process of our thinking. In other words, we must be thinkers of our own thoughts and focus more on how we think rather than how we feel, since our feelings are just a printout of our thoughts anyhow. By asking ourselves what action we can take for a better result we are then able to prevent undesirable outcomes and rise above the victim role. Rescripting our lives begins with ownership.

The Best Predictor of Future Success Is Past Success

Bill Brooks, CEO of The Brooks Group and author of *The New Science of Selling and Persuasion*, learned about ownership from his fourteen years of experience as a college football coach. He made it clear that we need to distinguish between perceived self-limits and real self-limits. Bill, who is shorter than I am, realized his goals to be in the NBA were just not in the cards. He also reversed the concept that motivation drives success, stating that success drives motivation, which is exactly why I so strongly encourage parents to get their kids hooked on winning at an early age.

I don't care if it's just winning the relay race or a game of Chinese checkers, no child passively vegetating before a TV gets hooked on winning, for only the actors you watch are the winners. Notice I said "actors" which has the word "act" in it. It is action and activity that gives the rewards that feel good and motivate us to achieve the next level. You do the math. The best predictor of future success is past success. Champions also never lose hope, which is why they never lose. "Hope is about expecting a positive outcome. You're dead in the water without it."

Bill gave credit to his mentor and high school football coach Jim Combs, who did not receive New Jersey coach of the year, five undefeated seasons in a row, and nineteen championships without some skill at developing confidence, competence, and team synergy. He recalled Jim's emphasis on preparation, discipline, confidence, and a belief in one's abilities as well as system thinking. Bill's formula is simple. "No rules of success will work unless you do." He admits to being a strong capitalist with a social work background, which is hopefully not an oxymoron, but confirms that his inner drive is to never say I didn't do my best. Because you become like those with whom you associate, Bill suggested becoming a copycat of those you hold in awe.

Beyond attitude, winners seemed to have a very different perception of problems, challenges, and would-be obstacles. Don Holzworth, the CEO of Constella Group, admitted that his company rose to greatness only after he sought coaching and transitioned his mindset from entrepreneur to CEO. Constella consistently receives the Platinum Rule Award for Best Places to Work. Unlike many of the other winners who were interviewed, Don did not have a vision of big success at an early age. However, he did share the common quality of a strong work ethic, discipline, and the desire to win. Don also had strong parental support and great role modeling. He never perceived undesired results with any disappointment or sense of defeat or failure, but rather thrived on the challenge as another mountain to climb or problem to solve. He obviously did not internalize the undesired results, but rather perceived such events very objectively with a healthy detachment that allowed him to maintain a positive attitude, personal strength, and psychological resilience. By not squandering his energies on negative self-talk or "kick me" behaviors, he maintained a high level of creative energy to not only problem solve but to move forward with renewed vigor and vision. Not unlike Paul Hamm's disappointing first performance on the parallel bars in the 2004 summer Olympics, there was never a sense of defeat or throwing in the towel. But rather continued hope, trust, and belief in oneself and one's ability to beat the odds.

The Secret to Success Is No Secret

Another man who knows no defeat is Lee Iacocca, the CEO of the Chrysler Corporation, who transformed a dying company into a booming success by leading a fight for business survival. The son of Italian immigrants, Lee Iacocca rose spectacularly through the ranks of the Ford Motor Company to become its president, but then got knocked down from the top just eight years later in a devastating power play that almost shattered him. Instead of getting mad, Lee got even. The tough-talking, straight-shooting businessman is seen by many as the living embodiment of the American dream.

His secret for success is really no secret. "I learned about the strength you can get from a close family life. I learned to keep going even in bad times. I learned not to despair even when my world was falling apart. I learned that there are no free lunches. And I learned about the value of hard work. In the end, you've got to be productive. That's what made this country great – and that's what's going to make us great again." No matter what country you are from, Lee's words of advice fits all people in all places.

Lee admits his instinct for marketing was learned from his father, the ultimate promoter, who did very well with restaurants, movie theaters, and real estate to create a fair amount of wealth. Mark Victor Hansen and Robert Allen, authors and financial gurus who recommend multiple streams of income, would smile kindly on Lee's father's diversified business ventures. When the Great Depression hit, all was lost. His mother and all family members pitched in to merely survive while drawing strength from their belief in God. He recalled the value of the Catholic confession forcing him to continually examine his life and be accountable for his behaviors, while weighing out right from wrong. Although I am not Catholic, I sure would like to bring back this self-examination ritual for all people of all faiths.

Lee admits the Depression turned him into a materialist and connected a few dots in deciding at that point to be a millionaire, which was a lot of money back in those days. There is power in the moment of decision. I personally endorse Lee's lessons and even as a member of the working rich, Lee still invests conservatively, eats leftovers, and does not spend money he does not have, with one exception—a loan of $1.2 billion to save Chrysler.

Why Walk When You Can Run

Obviously Lee's parents were great mentors. He recalls his father's little homilies about the ways of the world and reminded him that life has its ups and downs and we all have to accept a bit of misery and sorrow. His father always encouraged Lee to move on to tomorrow and that once again the sun's gonna shine. President Clinton's mother referred to rain as liquid sunshine, which also reminds us that the one thing we can always control is our perception of reality and how we choose to look at outside events. Lee's father accepted nothing less than one performing up to their potential and lived each moment to the fullest. In fact when he golfed, he would *run* after the ball he had just hit. When Lee reminded his father that golf was a game of walking, his father replied, "Why walk when you can run?"

Sir Richard Branson, founder of the Virgin companies, certainly lives up to his potential. Branson declared that he simply has so much fun starting companies that he seems to lose sight of the risk factors, which take second place. Branson has 150 companies that are all showing a profit in spite of having no prior experience in any of them. His favorite is Virgin Atlantic Airlines. To prevent corporate stagnation due to decision-making paralysis, Branson runs Virgin as a series of businesses to keep the process fluid. Whether it is Michael Jordan returning to basketball, or Richard Branson continually experimenting with new business arenas, the refrain is the same: "I love the game" or "I love what I do."

In his autobiography *Losing my Virginity*, Branson reports that his mother was determined to make her children independent, and as children they were always encouraged to have an opinion, not suppressed with, "Children should be seen and not heard." Controlling parents stifle independent thinking and thinking period, which may be why it was recently announced that we have a bumper crop of people who are life incompetent.

Overindulgent Negligence

To teach stamina and direction, Richard recalls his Mum dropping him off a few miles from home when he was only four years old and instructed him to find his own way home across the fields. There were continual challenges, more physical than academic. There was not only endless family support and love, but an identity of who they were as a family. His Granny never stopped learning until she died at the age of 99. They were definitely not watching 26 hours of TV every week, which is the average viewing time in North America. In fact, they did not even own a TV. However, Mum always found work for him and his siblings and she was always thinking of ways to make money—a lesson Branson learned well.

Leadership was well modeled and the family had a great sense of teamwork, with a priority placed on putting other people first, which explains the legacy of service in the Virgin companies. The boarding school he attended demanded discipline and results or beatings were the consequence, which I would not personally advocate, but discipline—yes. Branson's successes are a clear reflection of the challenges, demands, and expectations lovingly bestowed upon him by his parents. Don't sabotage your child's potential success with overindulgent negligence. As parents we are coaches, mentors, and spiritual guides responsible for providing an environment that encourages growth and being a bit better each and every day. Overprotection conveys a message of doubt and thus depletes confidence and self esteem. Remember, Alexander the Great was conquering the world by age 29, and nowadays "twixters," children who don't want to grow up, don't even leave the nest by that age.

We Take Bigger Steps When We Walk with Giants

Loral Langemeier, founder of Live Out Loud and author of *Guerilla Wealth,* teaches people how to create wealth and explains how winners think *differently.* They think BIG. They think YES. They think POSSIBLE. They also surround themselves with BIGGER and BETTER people to create a sphere of influence that challenges you and also provides a solid role model for achieving more. When we walk with giants we take bigger steps to keep up the pace. I know when I went downhill skiing with my sons I tried the black diamonds only because they did, and it has all been "downhill" ever since, or shall we say, "bunny hill." Mike Schanhofer, who has taken his Luxemburg-Casco girls basketball team to five Wisconsin State Championships, has these high school girls play routinely with young men who were college athletes to elevate their playing level. Like Loral, Schanhofer is all about action and results. To learn the plays by heart, he has the girls dribble, pass, and throw free throws blind-folded.

Loral has also created the RALT Model which stands for Results, Action, Language, and Thinking. She demonstrates the vicious cycle of how your thinking influences your language, which commits your actions. Your reactions thus produce your results, which directs your thinking. We often look at what we have or have not done as confirmation of what we can or cannot do.

Decisive Language Breeds Decisive Action and Expansive Results

Mark Victor Hansen, coauthor of the *Chicken Soup for the Soul* series, makes his eye for opportunity obvious when he commented, "There are more opportunities in one day that come into my life than I can do for the rest of my life." Loral confirms that when you commit to your goal you trigger decisive thinking and thus speak decisively and use decisive language which breeds decisive action and creates expansive results.

Loral cautions against use of the word "if," which is limiting, and encourages use of the word "when," which is decisive. Other decisive words such as "I will," "I won't," "yes," "no," are recommended while "can" and "can't" are about capability and have nothing to do with decisiveness.

Obviously capability is often a gift that for many remains unopened. For example, Darryl Strawberry, a very talented baseball player once with the New York Mets, chose to sabotage his success with a drug addiction that made jail his home rather than home plate. Certainly Freddie Prinze, John Belushi, Sandra Dee, Elvis Presley, and Kurt Cobain are other examples of how talent and success demand wisdom in knowing how to respond to our personal successes without losing ourselves in the process. Too often power and money become intoxicants that derail our superstars from their original goodness and innocence. They may lack a key ingredient of true leaders – the indomitable will.

Winners Never Quit: The Indomitable Will of Leaders

Robert (Dusty) Staub, author of *The Heart of Leadership* and *The 7 Acts of Courage*, offered this synopsis of how winners and leaders think differently.

1. They have indomitable "will." They are unconquerable, and when knocked down, they get back up and never, ever quit.

2. They are focused and have a profound sense of going for the gold and knowing where it is to be found. They are offensive and always moving "toward" their destiny rather than wasting their energy in a defensive mode where their goal is to avoid losing and getting hurt.

3. They encourage the hearts of others and serve people. Albert Schweitzer obviously agrees. "I do not know who you are, but I do know this. You will not find true happiness until you find a way to serve others."

4. They celebrate the deep mystery of life and have a deep-rooted optimism. They are religious and/or spiritual and have a faith in something greater than themselves, whether that faith is in God or destiny. They trust their intuition and are strengthened by their connection to the Source that lies within them through prayer, meditation, and reflection. Albert Einstein confessed that he knew far more than he could have known and simply used logic to prove it.

Dusty explained how we often abandon ourselves by doing what is safe, easy, or what pleases others rather than remaining true to ourselves and those who trust us most. As we make our brain a servant to our heart we discover our own magnificence. Certainly Mother Teresa, Gandhi, Oprah, Mary Kay Ash, and Joshua Chamberlain, brigadier general in the Civil War, all demonstrated this heart-centeredness in their actions that were always focused on doing the right thing. Chamberlain, a college professor who spoke seven languages and four-time governor of Maine, was not the typical front-line military leader, but may have been the decisive figure in the Civil War. He did not abandon himself and his beliefs that slavery was evil and that the Union should remain indivisible and thus followed his heart to take up arms and led a badly beaten army reporting seventy-five percent casualties and another one hundred twenty mutineers who had lost all hope and chose to abandon themselves and their beliefs.

Winners are leaders who influence, empower, and enlighten others as Chamberlain did when he inspired those who had given up to follow their hearts and continue the fight. Chamberlain lead his meager army of two hundred men down the hill with empty guns, as they had run out of ammunition, and captured five hundred Confederate soldiers which was a turning point in the Civil War. Chamberlain showed love, honor, and respect to the defeated Confederate soldiers upon their surrender. Champions are compassionate and honor others, whether in defeat or victory, because they first respect themselves.

Not What You Think but How You Think

Bruce Bell, a major in the U.S. Marine Corps, and senior account executive with CBLPath, states Marines are still taught those admirable qualities of honor, respect, and loyalty. He referred to an observation made by Admiral Nimitz about the Marines as they fought at Iwo Jima sixty years ago where one in ten—almost 7,000 marines— were killed in a thirty-six day battle. Nimitz saw uncommon valor as a common virtue in the Marines. Bruce agreed there was a built-in sense of responsibility, honor, courage, and commitment to accomplish any mission and to risk their lives instinctually. He mentioned that while serving in Iraq, a young child fell into a rapidly moving river across from the airfield they were protecting. Without a moment's hesitation his colleague stripped himself of all body gear in an attempt to save the child unfortunately without success, but his heroism is part of the culture.

Emphasizing it's not what you think but how you think, Bruce shared the *OODA Loop* that is taught to the Marines. If you process information more rapidly and act decisively, you "out-think" the enemy and win. Winning in the Marines may be the difference between life and death. However the same principles can be applied in our personal and business lives for raising our level of excellence.

O   – Observe
O   – Orientate
D   – Decide on action
A   – Act

Bruce added that when he looks at a challenge, he gets a broad view to be all encompassing, but then quickly extrapolates the key factors that contribute to a solution. With 80% certainty, he moves forward and takes action. If one waits for 100% certainty, the opportunity is lost.   After serving in Iraq, Bruce is certain that the desire for freedom is innate, although cultural conditioning and fear can act as a stun gun. The human spirit, however, is silently sustained until it is safe to speak, or even when it's not. Obviously the life-threatening choice to vote in Iraq's recent elections broke the silence for 60% of its people.

A Champion Is the Winner of the Winners

Now I know why Bruce's boss William Curtis, the CEO and Chairman of CBLPath, feels confident hiring Marines who come with core values and training that contribute to excellence. Since my own company's mission is "changing the way the world thinks—one mind at a time," I am in awe of Bill's ability to think, process, and strategize. With his degree in philosophy rather than business, I am convinced business schools need to make philosophy a requirement.

In my seminars on whole-brain thinking, I mention that some people have a lot of both left brain and right brain, and others may have nothing of either! With CBLPath's 500% growth rate in just over a year, Bill is one that has a lot of both right and left-brain resources. CBLPath is Bill's fourth company which certainly suggests he is a right-brain visionary and communicator. However, Bill also admits to being a stickler for details, organization, and analysis, which are the talents of left-brain wiring. Bill felt that many people succeeded in spite of themselves, and others with a strong sense of commitment can accomplish great things. Like Dr. Petty, Bill gave favoritism to the "how we're wired" theory, and felt that being a great team player is part of a person's personal makeup.

Seeing leadership skills as learned, Bill feels that leadership is innate, commenting that visionary people are not necessarily good leaders. Since leadership is not about obedience but rather followership, a true leader must therefore have more than the vision, but also the ability to get the team to participate in it. Getting people to follow directions is obedience and not true followership. Although humble, Bill is a champion leader of a team that allows him to leverage the efforts of many. Together, they all rise above. Bill breathes synergy and probably wrote The Law of Reciprocity for as he gives wholeheartedly to his team, he also receives his strength and inspiration from them as well. He sees the company, not himself, as the true champion.

If you are dishonest, without a strong work ethic, self-absorbed, and seeking what you can get rather than contribute, don't waste your time applying at CBLPath. Bill only hires people who really care beyond themselves. He seeks consistency in people having a strong ethical core, but then looks for diversity in thinking styles and abilities. He always tries to "hire up," i.e. hire people better than himself. He has a simple but effective method for recruiting a high-performance work team by getting answers to the following three questions:

1. Who is the person—core values and priorities

2. What have they done—track record of success

3. What can the do for us—attitude, skills, experience

He likes people who have drive and wake up in the morning seeing the world around us as something to be conquered. Opportunity knocks incessantly; we just have to choose what knocks we want to respond to. Bill confidently knows he can identify and create more opportunities than there will ever be time to pursue. Thus, choosing the right opportunity is essential.

Bill sees a champion as the winner of the winners and the pinnacle of success. While winners seek to meet and exceed their expectations, champions contribute to a cause and make a difference in the lives of others. Good leaders will win and give themselves the opportunity to be a champion. Sometimes potential champions are not obvious. I am sure Bill's aunt is smiling for when he received three scholarships at his high school graduation, she responded, in a state of shock, "Bill, I never knew you were smart." (Compliment or insult—you be the judge.)

During my speaking tour in Russia, I was overwhelmed by the number of champions wanting to contribute and make a difference. Perhaps when we are silenced, we have a greater desire to speak. Nonna Barkhatova, Ph.D., is president of the National Association of Entrepreneurs and the Small Business Development Center in Novosibirsk, Russia. Upon completion of her doctoral studies in England and research in Hungary, Nonna returned to integrate the business practices of the western world into the Russian marketplace. Obviously, she is not easily intimidated by large goals, such as reshaping Russian business ethics and strategies. Feeling the excitement of new beginnings, Vladimir Tonkonog, a 32-year old entrepreneur, has already started five successful companies and exhibits the confidence of Donald Trump. Ludmila Vorobeva, a vibrant 65-year old retired engineer, has enough energy to light up all of Russia. She is the embodiment of the X factors and indomitable will. Ludmila was born with optimism in her DNA and in any political environment, communism or capitalism, Ludmila radiates an inner joy that permeates all in her presence.

People with the X factors—charisma, chutzpah, exuberance, and grace—project a positive energy that radiates beyond the person who embodies it. Charismatic people are natural "attractors" who get others to synchronize to them, according to Carlin Flora in a report in *Psychology Today*. Carlin explains, "With proper support, even a shy wallflower can muster the courage to be provocative, but people with true gumption have life experiences that force them to use their natural boldness to break boundaries…People with *joie de vivre* are like windup dolls that never run down; they are passionate explorers who view their work as play… Positive thinking can be taught, but passionate exuberance is something you're born with. Grace is the quietest of the X-factors, perhaps the only one in which star power never threatens to overshadow substance. Wisdom is also associated with benevolence, and it is in warm, compassionate individuals that we often see grace."

CHAPTER EIGHT

BREAKTHROUGH THINKING: THE DNA OF SUCCESS

> *"To think is to practice brain chemistry. The possibility of stepping into a higher plane is quite real for everyone. It requires no force or effort or sacrifice. It involves little more than changing our ideas about what is normal."*
> **Deepak Chopra**

Before we can develop breakthrough thinking we must rethink our thinking and go beyond what we think to how we think. In my first book, *Why Cats Don't Bark,* I revealed the power of our intuitive intelligence and gut guidance to unleash our PowerZone. In *Sparks of Genius* by Robert and Michele Root-Bernstein, they cite examples of many accomplished people who make reference to the "aha" experience or intuition being the spark to their achievements.

Eureka! The Problem Is the Answer

Barbara McClintock, a Nobel Prize winner in genetics, stated back in 1930 while at Cornell University she shouted, "Eureka, I have it! I have the answer! I know what this thirty percent sterility is." When her colleagues asked her to prove it, she realized that she had no idea how to explain her insight. Decades later McClintock explained, "When you suddenly see the problem, something happens that you have the answer – before you are able to put it into words. It is all done subconsciously. This has happened many times to me, and I know when to take it seriously. I'm so absolutely sure. I don't talk about it, I don't have to tell anybody about it, I'm just sure this is it."

The reason Barbara may not have told anyone about her knowing is, like Bob Dylan, someone will kill it. Jack Schwarz, author of *Human Energy Systems*, said that at the moment of conflict and indecision we simultaneously have the answer. It just often takes years for us to be aware of it, accept it, and act on it. How often have you known what you needed to do but just did not have the guts to act on it? For example, in many marriages people are often divorced emotionally for years before they actually file the papers or correct the relationship. We so often deceive ourselves and live with our own lies.

The Heart Has Its Reasons That Reason Cannot Know

Blaise Pascal, the French philosopher and mathematician, confirmed the feeling of knowing without being able to give a logical explanation. "The heart has its reasons that reason cannot know." Carl Frederich Gauss agreed that intuition often led him to ideas he could not immediately prove. "I have had my results for a long time: but I do not yet know how I am to arrive at them."

Claude Bernard, the founder of modern physiology, wrote that everything purposeful in scientific thinking began with a feeling. "Feeling alone guides the mind." The famous painter Pablo Picasso made a similar confession. "I don't know in advance what I am going to put on canvas any more than I decide beforehand what colors I am going to use...Each time I undertake to paint a picture I have a sensation of leaping into space. I never know whether I shall fall on my feet. It is only later that I begin to estimate more exactly the effect of my work." The effect of Picasso's work is a painting that sold in 2004 for 104 million dollars. That is landing on your feet!

I Know That I Know What I Don't Know

The Bernsteins also cited composer Igor Stravinsky who found that imaginative activity began with some inexplicable appetite, some "intuitive grasp of an unknown entity already possessed but not yet intelligible." Isabel Allende, a Latin American novelist, described a similarly vague sense propelling her work and reported, "Somehow inside me – I know that I know where I am going. I know that I know the end of the book even though I don't know it. It's so difficult to explain." (I might add that it is so difficult to explain only in a logical, linear sense.)

Michelangelo said, "In every rock of marble I see a statue, I merely chisel away so that others can see what I already know." Those winners and champions who have chosen to make a difference in the arts seem to be translators of the abstract thought into the concrete reality of beauty for sensory enjoyment and pleasure. Those who are scientists astutely observe, synthesize, and integrate abstract concepts and translate them into tangibles that improve our lives and the planet. Robert and Michele summarized their findings with the following synopsis.

> ...Indeed, scientist and artist are kin, for their insights begin in the same realm of feeling and intuition and emerge into consciousness through the same creative process. And that is the point. It is too easy to look at the diverse things people produce and to describe their differences. Obviously a poem is not a mathematical formula, and a novel is not an experiment in genetics. Composers clearly use a different language from that of visual artists, and chemists combine very different things than do playwrights. But neither is all scientific thinking monolithic (physics is not biology) or all art the same (a sculpture is not a collage or a photograph).
>
> To characterize people by the different things they make is to miss the universality of how they create. For at the level of the creative process, scientists, artists, mathematicians, composers, writers, and sculptors use a common set of what we call 'tools for thinking." Including emotional feelings, visual images, bodily sensations, reproducible patterns, and analogies. And all imaginative thinkers learn to translate ideas generated by these subjective thinking tools into public languages to express their insights, which can then give rise to new ideas in others' minds. This new 'logic'—perhaps Ulan's term 'metalogic,' is more appropriate—can prove nothing; rather, it generates novel ideas and conceptions, with no assurance of their validity or utility. This kind of thinking, as yet unstudied and unaccounted for by modern theories of mind, is nonverbal, nonmathematical, and non-symbolic inasmuch as it does not belong to a formal language of communication. Nevertheless, our challenge here is to describe and understand this metalogic of feelings, images, and emotions. At present, the closest concept we have to such a metalogic is the vague one of intuition. Einstein said, 'Only intuition, resting on sympathetic understanding, can lead to insight; the

daily effort comes from no deliberate intention or program, but straight from the heart.'

His colleague Henri Poincare, perhaps the greatest mathematician of the late nineteenth century, wrote in Science and Method, 'It is by logic that we prove, but by intuition that we discover.... Logic teaches us that on such and such a road we are sure of not meeting an obstacle; it does not tell us which is the road that leads to the desired end. For this it is necessary to see the end from afar, and the faculty that teaches us to see is intuition. Without it, the geometrician would be like a writer well up in grammar but destitute of ideas.

Physicist Max Planck put it even more simply: ' the scientist needs an artistically creative imagination.' Indeed, scientist and artist are kin, for their insights begin in the same realm of feeling and intuition and emerge into consciousness through the same creative process. Not enough recognize the cross-disciplinary nature of intuitive tools for thinking. No matter how expressed, the perspectives of Gell-Mann and Gabo, Stravinsky and Nicolle converge on the same point, aptly made by Arthur Koestler in his seminal book. ' The Art of Creation: Newtons's apple and Cezanne's apple are discoveries more closely related than they seem.' Both require reperceiving and reimagining the world from basic perceptual feelings and sensations. All of these people, whether they are doing artistic work or scientific work, are trying to solve a problem. French physician Armand Trousseau agreed: 'All science touches on art; all art has its scientific side. The worst scientist is he who is not an artist; the worst artist is he who is no scientist'. Painter Susan Rosenberg describes her process of painting as 'really visceral,' and another painter, Bridget Riley describes her paintings as 'intimate dialogue[s].'

I Go Where I Am Being Pushed

Someone who translates abstract concepts into tangible and breath-taking art is Beverly Carrick, an artist from Bakersfield, California. Like Bob Dylan, Beverly sees her talent as a God-given gift and feels her life has been directed. "Some things are meant to be. I go with where I am being pushed." I was mesmerized by Beverly's art when I had stepped into an art gallery in Sante Fe, New Mexico, and her art not only speaks to you, it breathes! In fact, Beverly herself described art as a living thing as opposed to a calendar that expires. Those words made me feel so justified in the artwork I have purchased at times when my money should have gone to more practical purchases. Champions truly do connect with their medium and their craft but also with the people who understand and appreciate it. As she put it, "My work is not done when I finish it, but when someone else appreciates it."

One never knows where they might get their inspiration. Beverly got hers from when she lived in an ugly mining town, but noticed that when the sun would shine on the weeds of the dry desert, they would glisten and turn to gold which made her aware of the impact of lighting. I have never seen an artist use light to create such an illuminating effect as Beverly. She recalls when in the sixties she was doing junk art for $12.00 for the standard 24x36 painting. She was never insulted that the frames were always worth more than her talents, but her unhappiness in her first marriage motivated her to become financially independent and leave the relationship.

Beverly's gifts actually began with dance. Her dreams of being a ballerina were interrupted by bone cancer at the age of 12 that resulted in her leg being amputated. This was standard treatment in 1940 before chemotherapy. With her unsinkable Molly Brown spirit, she continued to ride her bike, horses, and even danced with a prosthetic device that resembled a tree stump. In fact she was walking just two weeks after losing her leg and had made a decision not to be depressed but to only look forward.

In discovering her talent and passion with the brush, she regained her sense of being "special," for losing a leg certainly can affect one's self esteem, especially at age 12. Self-esteem requires more than another's love, but also a sense of competency and mastery in various activities. Her alcoholic husband found humor in pushing her down when her prosthesis was off, but she solved that problem by moving forward and having twenty memorable years with her second husband. Bash on regardless! (This is a British military term meaning find a way to keep moving forward.)

Like so many of the extraordinary people I have interviewed, reading and being read to was also a pleasant memory for Beverly who reports having the Greek classics read to her at age 7, when most children have their noses in comic books. Beverly feels you are born with the "stuff" and what you do with it is your choice. Although well beyond the *usual* retirement age, Beverly is still in the process of perfecting her art and commits at least four hours a day to that end. Again the question of retirement brought about a defensive, "No," explaining that she would lose her primary expression of enjoyment. Consistent with her "always look for the good attitude," Beverly commented that by having cancer and losing her leg she diverted her talent from dancing to art which doesn't come with an age limitation.

It Is Not How You Start Out but How You Finish

Another artist Jeffrey Ferrell, who resides in Maryland, has the same commitment to continual renewal and constant improvement. Unlike the athletes interviewed who constantly measured their improvement by the performance of their competition, the artists judged themselves by their own critical eye, where you cannot cheat. There are no steroids or muscle building drugs. The truth cannot be denied.

With artists who do not have a timed measurement of success as a runner, the goal is more to "connect" with others who might understand their message and method of translation. They work alone, but their emotional connections are strong. Jeffrey's philosophy, which reflects his mentor and marketing guru Jay Abraham, is that: "It is not how you start out but how you finish." However, Jeffrey will never be finished, since for him, to stop doing and growing is to die. He confessed to always knowing he was different than the norm and chose to perceive it as being "special" rather than as a reject. It is not only how we look at things, but also how we look at ourselves. Inspiration is everywhere and often free or those who reach out. While many found their role models in books, Jeffrey found his at the National Museum of Art and is thankful to Paul Mellon whose generosity and contributions to that gallery made fine art available to all. Obviously our limiting belief systems and excuses are greater obstacles than limited talent or money.

After numerous rejections, Jeffrey's art now claims the National Gallery of Art as home. He does confess that there was that one person who really believed in him as he recalls his mother's convincing words, "You can do anything you want to do." My guess is that many still searching have not become clear on what it is they really want to do, for once one is clear on what it is they want, providence moves us in the direction of our destiny.

I think of Barbara Streisand's interview on *60 Minutes* where she admitted that she *knew* she would be a star even though her mother lovingly reminded her of her limitations—her nose—and her own stepfather told her she was too ugly for an ice cream cone. While having someone who truly believes in you is great support and encouragement, for those clear on their calling and soul's code, nothing gets in the way. Nothing!

The Effect of the Cause: Love – Truth – Beauty

Nothing gets in the way of the laws of cause and effect. In Einstein's theory of relativity, energy is the cause and the universe is the effect, according to The Father of American Tae Kwon Do, Grandmaster Jhoon Rhee. "It is logical to pose the question of 'why' when we want to find an answer to the ultimate reason of any matter in human affairs. For instance…the watch is clearly explained by the purpose it serves…to help us to know the time. What many or most of the world's philosophies do not or cannot do is to account for the existence of God in our universe."

Science has sought to satisfy the unfinished explanation of religion and to solve the eternal search of man for that thing: that entity, that life force which is eternally permanent and indestructible beyond our perceptual world…. Einstein's answer was then, and our answer is today: energy. Energy replaced all other concepts as being the permanent force of life in this formula.

This universe consists of mineral, plant, and animal kingdoms that contain characteristics of "Truth in Mineral, Beauty in Plant, and Love in the Animal Kingdom." Animal feelings are mostly instinctive, while the most distinctive characteristic of an animal is love. Since we have found the three characteristics of Truth, Beauty, and Love in the universe, which are the Effect, there must be the three characteristics of Truth, Beauty, and Love in the Energy, which are the Cause. These three universal human values of truth, beauty, and love are the three special fabrics needed to construct a Utopian society where everyone is happy with every breath of life for everyone. When we are truthful, we are happy; when we are happy, we are beautiful in our hearts and in the mind and spirit of those around us.

Beyond the universal values mentioned by Mr. Rhee, I want to add freedom. People fight wars and die for freedom whether it be freedom of thought, freedom of religion, or free to live life one's very own way. It is the freedom to live and enjoy one's truth which, like God, may be difficult to account for due to its ethereal nature. Champions were determined to have the freedom to do what they loved doing, i.e. their passion, and exercise their truth to experience the beauty and joy of living life to the fullest whether it be to summit Mt. Everest, win the marathon, create a company, write a book that changes lives, or be the best darn parent in the world. Winning is being all that one can be.

Innovative Thinking: The Currency of the Future

Dan Burrus, founder of Burrus Research, certainly exercises his truth and freedom to do what he loves doing. Some people talk about thinking out of the box but Dan Burrus, author of *TechnoTrends*, lives out of the box. In fact Dan has no boxes! His expertise is how to use technology to go beyond the competition. Dan's solution is rather than compete, companies should use technology to change the rules with honesty and integrity.

Three cheers for his mother who taught him to be observant. She continually asked him questions about his surroundings to give early childhood stimulation. Unfortunately, most parents have delegated stimulation to the television, which doesn't ask questions nor does it provide applause and encouragement. Kudos likewise to his father, an engineer, with a scientific mind who talked in adult, scientific terms to his children. Children learn "baby talk" because that's the silly lingo they are taught by their parents.

Another gifted guy with lots of activity in both hemispheres of the brain, Dan has a science background and has built robots and ultra lights (a hang glider with a small engine). A big-picture thinker, Dan produced award-winning films when he was just out of college; played seven different instruments in a rock band; and still gets rave reviews from his work in art galleries. After starting five companies, two of which became national leaders within the first year, Dan shared his business wisdom by writing over a dozen books many being bestsellers in the US and abroad. Power follows ideas, and Dan is an idea generator. (It's amazing what one can accomplish when they entertain themselves with something other than TV and video games.)

As the first undergraduate student in the nation to direct the Federal Research Grant, he had his college professors coming to him begging to work in his grant. While the professors were accomplished and decorated with titles and letters such as Ph.D., Dan was a young, ambitious man with endless ideas. You decide what works.

The Chant of Champs: Making a Difference

Although well paid as a strategic advisor, Dan states that money has never been a motivating force. "Do what you love doing and the money will follow" has definitely been the mantra of this accomplished group. In fact, Dan had turned down well-paying, easy jobs and instead chose to work in the inner city where he felt he could do more good and make a difference. Making a difference is definitely the chant of champs.

By creating his own playing field, developing a new game, and changing the rules of the old game, Dan differentiates himself and leverages his uniqueness by maximizing his natural gifts and creating an environment where there is no competition and no odds to beat. If you are in a competitive environment, change the rules of how you are competing—with honesty and integrity, of course. He noted that Marriott put computers in their hotel kitchens to ensure that room service orders were delivered right on time down to the minute. They changed the way people had thought about customer service, since previously we all had been somewhat accepting of the order being delivered *close* to the requested time.

Take Your Biggest Problem and Skip It

A unique system of problem solving, Dan suggests you take your biggest problem and skip it. For example, Dan lives in Wisconsin, and brutally cold winters are his biggest problem so he skips it. He spends February in Hawaii. I think too often we waste a lot of energy fighting a boss, relationship, or situation which could be better resolved by skipping it, jumping over it, or rising above it. What situations are you dealing with that you might resolve by applying this quantum leap theory?

Eli Lilly used this principle successfully when they couldn't pay for the thousands of researchers needed to solve a problem. They published the problem on a website in twelve languages and offered to pay for the solution which was offered by 1,500 researchers who successfully solved the problem. Brilliant! Creativity is not only effective and efficient it is impossible to survive in our competitive global economy without it. It is the core of business success, and innovative thinking *is* the currency of the future. Eureka! is not just an enlightening moment but should be a business strategy. Mary Kay Ash, founder of Mary Kay Cosmetics, has a suggestion similar to Dan's idea of just skipping it. "For every failure, there's an alternative course of action. You just have to find it. When you come to a roadblock, take a detour."

While Dan draws strength from his optimistic attitude, a pessimist anticipates failure and thus never rolls the dice. Hope grounded in reality is a powerful force for all of us. Dan's concept, *Futureview*, explains how we create our future. "How you view the future shapes how you act in the present and how you act in the present shapes your future. Therefore, your future view will determine the future you." (By the way, rose-colored glasses are permissible.) Incidentally, Dan's response to the retirement question was, "From what? I have never had a job. I'm not working."

Change Your Internal Map – Interest Is Not Enough

John Assaraf, founder of the Cloning of Success workshop and author of the bestseller, *The Street Kid's Guide to Having It All*, also helps people create a more successful future by unleashing untapped potential. John decided to rise above his family's poverty, his health problems, and his role in the street gangs of Montreal. Although he had loving parents, he left home at age 19 to seek out powerful mentors who taught him well: he has since started several lucrative, successful companies that could fill this entire chapter.

Since habits are a thousand times more powerful than desires, John emphasizes the power of the "why" and the neuro-reconditioning process. To change a behavior having an interest in changing is simply not enough. Changing our internal map and commitment is essential to energizing the forces of change. Emotions create an energy intensity that moves us to new behavior patterns, which is why a significant emotional experience will instantaneously create new neuro-pathways in the brain. For example, people who may have lost a loved one due to smoking, drinking, or obesity, may instantly change their lifestyle and health habits. They may leave a stressful job or relationship, start exercising, quit smoking, and begin to eat real food which would not be accomplished with just an interest or professed New Year's resolution.

Unfortunately, others will begin to smoke or drink excessively after the loss of a loved one because when we are experiencing extreme stress we shift from our creative mind to the instinctual brain and resort back to bad habits still stored in our unconscious mind. Our ability to store and process knowledge and create new thoughts, connections, and ideas is virtually unlimited. The ability for the brain to constantly change is referred to as brain plasticity. Although once thought that geniuses had more brain cells, we now know that they simply have better connections. Autism is an example where the child's neuro-connections within the brain are reduced and thus they are not able to effectively express themselves.

Since 83% of our actions are rooted in the unconscious mind, to be successful you may want to spend less time on your finger nails or polishing your car and more time on understanding how you can put your mind to work—efficiently! For example, thoughts in your conscious mind race at a top speed of 140 miles per hour, while thoughts and impulses on the unconscious level rocket at a breathtaking 28 miles *per second* and processes information 24/7. Maybe time management gurus need to look at brain boosters to give more results in less time. My character building program for children, *Wings for Wishes*, puts your child's brain into overdrive and programs them at an early age for values, success, and healthy life choices.

Belief More Than Truth Creates Our Habits

John states that more than truth, our beliefs will create our habits. Beliefs create a feeling of certainty and thus we find and seek only evidence that matches up and supports our predetermined belief. This is exactly why our self-image is crucial to positive change and illustrates why most people gain back the weight they may have lost. They forget that change occurs from the inside or "insight" out, and therefore a change in one's self-image is essential for any permanent change. His formula for success is as follows:

> **Belief + Experience x Repetition = Habit**
>
> **Habit + Experience x Repetition = Conviction**

With an emphasis on universal laws, John teaches that we are co-creating with an Infinite Intelligence or God, and thus our power comes from tapping into a source available to all of us. In the 14th century, Leonardo da Vinci tapped into images of submarines, helicopters, and parachutes, which was just a bit before scientists manifested the same realities. Ralph Ellison describes power in these words. "Power doesn't have to show off. Power is confident, self-assuring, self-starting and self-stopping, self-warming and self-justifying. When you have it, you know it."

John summed up the seven power factors of success as follows:

1. Persistence

2. Attitude

3. Discipline

4. Vision

5. Purpose

6. Focus

7. Action

Power is about energy. Thoughts and feelings are energy. In fact, *everything* is energy. We will often meet someone we like and say, "I love your energy" or "I get good vibes." If you choose negative thoughts, you create a negative energy field and begin to align yourself with that frequency, just as your positive thoughts will attract positive intelligence and energy. It is based on your interpretation of the vibration you sense within yourself and others. Your brain is the switch box and the control center for the realities you create. Your surroundings reflect your own perception of reality. Thus, if you don't like what you see in the people around you at home or at work, look first at yourself to change it. The only reality is our own.

The fact that we can store six million volumes of *The Wall Street Journal* in our brain reflects the ever-expanding magnitude of the mind. With one cell being more complex than if we were to turn on every phone in the world, and with 100 billion neurons ready to fire and move us forward, the power we have within us unfortunately scares most people into their own defeat and demise. We so often sabotage our own potential and success quotient with fears, doubts, and worries based on a negative imagination or experiences that resulted from the same limited thinking. Check your habits of thinking, for they are the forecast of your future. Aristotle said many years ago, "We are what we repeatedly do. Excellence, then, is not an act, but a habit." We must not trust our success to accidents, but rather ourselves and our actions.

Human Acceptance Code

I accept myself as a worthwhile person of unique value, talents, abilities, and potential for great accomplishment in a world full of possibilities.

I accept that the only limitations I have are self-imposed and can be changed merely by changing my habits of thinking and feeling.

I accept that I can become the self-fulfilling prophecy of my highest dreams and aspirations for happiness and accomplishment, by believing in myself and my ultimate victory over circumstance.

I accept that each day is an unrepeating miracle, a fresh start, a chance to live fully and with enthusiasm now, in this world and in my present circumstances.

I accept that I can control my moods, feelings and emotions, and that the only conflict that exists, is that conflict which I allow to exist, that I can change my life merely by changing the way I feel about or react to daily circumstances.

I accept that to be able to love others, I must first learn to love and accept myself, and then project those same feelings into the lives of others.

I accept that I can live in peace, harmony and fulfillment in my life, by training myself to maintain a positive attitude toward all persons and circumstances of my life, allowing nothing to upset the balance of my own little universe.

Keith Frost – 1975

CHAPTER NINE

DOING THE RIGHT THING: ACTION WITH INTEGRITY

> *"Life is either a daring adventure or nothing. To keep our faces toward change and behave like free spirits in the presence of fate is strength undefeatable."*
> **Helen Keller**

Rosa Parks certainly did not see fear as an obstacle when she sparked the flames of change in December of 1955 in Montgomery, Alabama. An African-American seamstress returning home from work, Rosa was riding the bus in the section reserved for blacks when some whites got on. With all seats taken in the white section, the white bus driver asked her and three others to give up their seats, which none of them did. After threatening remarks from the bus driver, all relinquished their seats except for Rosa whose courage led to a U.S. Supreme Court decision that desegregated buses across the nation. Rosa admits she was motivated by emotions rather than any well thought-out strategic plan. Feeling so outraged and weary of being unfairly pushed around throughout her life, her anger overruled her fears. Never underestimate the magic of one and the miracle of many.

Aristotle said, "Anyone can become angry—that is easy. But to be angry with the right person, to the right degree, at the right time, for the right purpose, and in the right way—that is not easy." Rosa chose the right target, in the right way, to the right degree, at the right time, for the right purpose. To recognize our profound feelings and act with precision requires patience, contemplation, and reflection that we all must integrate into our lives.

Light Always Overcomes Darkness

Marcia Steele, another African-American woman, continues in the spirit and chutzpah of Rosa Parks. With roots in Jamaica, Marcia grew up in a single-parent household but due to an enterprising mother she was not without opportunity. Marcia reflects on her achievements as due to the power of vision and belief, stating that if our beliefs are more powerful than our circumstances they will create our circumstances and results. She referred to the parable delivered by Jesus, "If your faith is the size of a mustard seed, you could move mountains." Marcia also emphasized focusing on *where* you want to go and *why* you want to go there without being sidetracked. Her favorite quote is, "If the lamp of your eye is dark, there is no hope." Marcia explained that our light is having a "why." She pointed out that light follows darkness and that light always overcomes the darkness. When there is light, there also is a shadow, where many may reside. But when they see the light they too will probably move out of their dimly lit space. We are nourished and energized by light, which is why even plants grow toward the sun.

Moving to New York City in the sixties, which was not a period of peace and tranquility, Marcia recalls being exposed to the "N word" for the first time in her life when Martin Luther King, Jr. had been assassinated. It was her second day on her respectable job in technology on Wall Street, although people mistook her for the cleaning lady. It was a rude awakening to discover what "being black" meant in America.

Three months later, Bobby Kennedy was assassinated during his campaign for president. She recalls being shocked in seeing more guns on each college campus than in the entire Jamaican militia. Paralyzed with fear, she found it difficult to venture out into the city's subways. Marcia also experienced prejudice as a woman in the male-dominated IT (Internet technology) world. These injustices, along with her sister's cancer, increased her desire to leave a legacy by creating her own company. Strategic Realities, Inc. has been empowering female executives since 1995. Nothing has held Marcia back, even two bouts with cancer: breast cancer in 2001 and ovarian cancer in 2004. She encourages others to gain their strength by literally keeping your head up and focusing on where you are going to avoid the potholes of life. Marcia cited John Wooden, one of the most successful college basketball coaches: "Do not let what you cannot do interfere with what you can do."

Fly Deep!

Marcia only focuses on what she can do, stating that her purpose in life is three-fold: to seek her God; to be a blessing to a huge amount of people; and to do significant work. She cited Jackie Kennedy Onassis' response to her driver's question while taking her to work one morning. The driver kindly asked Jackie why with all her wealth she continued to work. Her response was, "It is a privilege and duty."

It is our duty to serve and to be a blessing to others. It is a responsibility to contribute to this blessed land as long as we are taking from it. Participation is not optional, but we must continuously be in a dynamic exchange with the people and the earth we inhabit. Our lives are in our hands and our strength is in our five fingers. The first is faith, the second family, and the third is friends, followed by fitness and then funds or finance. It helped her overcome her challenges. You may wish to make it your source of strength as well.

In Marcia's presentation *Flying Deep*, she reflects on her younger years while walking the beaches of Jamaica and watching the seagulls diving for their food. The more ambitious seagulls would not settle for the dead fish washed upon the shore, but would rather fly deep down below the surface of the water where the fresh fish were swimming. The fresher fish provided more energy for the seagulls to fly even higher. Perhaps we all need to remember that the real gold, the jewels and rewards in our race to the top, is found below the surface—down deep within us. For our ideas to fly high we need to think deep. As we live in a global economy where most countries will be involved in "doing," the major players will provide the R&D, research and development, which requires deeper thinking and higher levels of innovation and creativity.

Marcia reminded us that immigrants come here with positive expectations of the American dream, while many of the American-born citizens give no thought to their dreams and aspirations and thus may often fall into the sea of mediocrity. Our founding fathers may have been so exceptionally successful and extraordinary in their endeavors because they too left Europe with a dream. They had a belief system and a "why," which gave their efforts the driving force of purpose where mediocrity was simply not acceptable. Have you compromised your dreams for the ease of mediocrity? How will you fly deep to rise above? Remember, dreams are not in a country, but in your heart.

Jim Rohn, philosopher and author, has not compromised his dreams at the expense of mediocrity. He sees neglect as the reason so many are not achieving their goals. Neglect is like an infection. Left unchecked it will spread throughout our entire system of disciplines and eventually lead to a complete breakdown of a potentially joy-filled and prosperous human life. Jim claims his success is a result of what he found easy to do, others found easy not to do. Everything we need is within our reach, but we simply neglect the opportunities. Jim also points out the self-defeating cycle of inactivity that leads to guilt that erodes self-confidence and in turn diminishes our activity level even more so. This further reduces results and thus shifts our attitude from positive to negative and on and on, leading us to defeat.

The Law of Accumulation states that everything accumulates over time, just as building a snowball starts small but grows as it accumulates millions of tiny snowflakes and thus gathers momentum. Certainly as you accumulate knowledge, you increase your value, and as you save money, it accumulates and attracts even more to add to your savings. Most people retire poor because they never initiated the process of accumulation. The third area where accumulation can create success and abundance is experience, which requires taking risks and moving out of one's comfort zone. Everything counts as a positive or negative in the ledger of life and integrity is the judge.

Become That to Which You Aspire

Muhammad Ali had no comfort zone; but only a power zone. By repeatedly proclaiming to be the greatest, his words created beliefs that propelled him to the top becoming the first man in heavyweight boxing history to win the crown three times. When we believe in something to the point of expectation our behavior changes. For example, if you really believe it will rain, you take an umbrella. You never know what sparks the flame. For Ali, born as Cassius Clay, it was having his bike stolen at age 12 and in his youthful rage he told the cop he would "whup" whoever stole his bike. The policeman, Joe Martin, fueled the flame when he replied, "You better learn to box first," and within weeks the 89-pound Cassius won his first bout. His style was to "dance like a butterfly, sting like a bee."

If we act the way we want to be, we will be the way we act. In the movie *Raging Bull*, Robert DeNiro played the role of Jake LaMotta, and after a thousand rounds of boxing for the film, he had literally become a boxer. Similarly, Gary Oldman, playing Beethoven in *Immortal Beloved*, actually became a pianist and Hilary Swank might have taken on Muhammad Ali as a boxer after so much practice in *Million Dollar Baby*. The same is true when victim roles are played. Janet Leigh stated she could not take a shower after playing the scene in Alfred Hitchcock's film, *Psycho*, where she was murdered while taking a shower.

Jim Valvano is most remembered as the North Carolina State University basketball coach who in 1983 convinced his underdog Wolfpack team they could overpower Houston in the NCAA Championship game, remembered as one of the biggest upsets in NCAA history. Jim understood the importance of mental and behavioral rehearsal, i.e. playing winning roles. Jim had his underdog team believe they were winners by having them bring out the ladder and have each team member cut the net as if they had just won the National Championship. Jim would have the last snip as they were cheered on by each other and looked out at an enthusiastic imaginary crowd until it manifested into reality.

Although Jim lost his fight with cancer at just 47, he had accomplished everything on his list and his spirit continues to inspire others with his legacy.   While a basketball commentator for ABC/ESPN, he formed the V Foundation for Cancer Research, which continues to grow and give others hope and treatment. Winners affect change even after the curtain call.

Liberace, a lavish pianist who had his own TV program before his passing, revealed that he too would "act as if" by playing to an empty audience except in his mind, but only until those images manifested into reality. Visualize your successes: seeing is believing, and believing is achieving. Being a champion is doing your homework and learning the lessons, for we are all students in the classroom of life. By "acting as if" and playing a variety of roles, we feel empowered and expand our social skills to more easily relate to diverse groups and increase our sphere of influence.

Like climbing a mountain, there are obstacles along the way and problems to solve. There are tradeoffs and compromises. The path is rarely paved in gold. Aron Ralston was literally caught between a rock and a hard place which made cutting off his hand to free his body a solution to the problem. If we can't we must; if we must we can. Another example of survival's strength is the man who was found drifting in the ocean fifteen days after the tsunami hit the Asian coast. He survived on coconuts and prayer, which may not be a balanced diet but it got him to the finish line.

Successful People Roll the Dice

Whether people are born high-risk or risk-averse is somewhat controversial, but clearly without taking risks there is no finish line. Dr. Charles Petty, a family humorist and President of Family Success Unlimited, believes we are wired or born with a high or low-risk tolerance, and successful people are those that tend to roll the dice. They trust that, "When you absolutely have to land that plane, there will be a runway—even if you can't see it sometimes," as explained by John Hamm, the director of Internet Capital Group.

Dr Petty explained that there are three types of intellect. One type is academic smarts, which is what we strongly reward in our educational system, especially in our grade schools and high schools. We even see it reflected in our bumper stickers, such as "I am the proud parent of an honor student." Another type is creativity or creative smarts that we tend not to reward in our educational systems; in fact we often penalize the child who colors out of the lines and creates a new path or system. They are reprimanded for breaking the rules. The third type of intellect is "street smarts" which is common in kids that become our "wheeler dealers" and often end up as the CEO of the company. No schmooze, you lose and they don't like losing. Charles referred to politicians as often possessing street smarts and added that it is an ability that cannot be taught and tends to be instinctual. As opposed to many others who believe that champions are made and not born, Dr. Petty leaned more toward how we are wired as the predominant factor in whom we become. He referred to those children who, like Elton John as a child, just sit at a piano and without any instruction begin to play beautiful music.

Dr. Petty is well wired which may have been motivated by the survival instinct. Charles was living on his own at age 15 after losing his mother to cancer at age 9, and then his father and brother who were killed in a car accident six years later. He had learned to survive by saying and doing the right thing and saying it gently. Charles admitted emotional pain can be a great teacher, if you're not destroyed by it. He defined hope as a wish of what might come true, and thus often leads to faith. However, it is belief that carries the power of conviction that propels action.

While some of the Olympians I interviewed found that one moment in time at the Olympics was worth the struggle to get there, Dr. Petty defined winners and champions as decent human beings who live a moral life and make contributions to their family, neighborhood, community, and workplace.

Be Authentic: To Thine Own Self Be True

Authenticity requires rolling the dice. When we violate our own truth, the body may go into a spontaneous rebellion that can ground us and guide us into a positive direction if we obey and heed the warning. Keith Varnum, author of *Living the Dream* and *Inner Coach: Outer Power,* is the founder of The Dream Workshops, where he helps people access their soul's blueprint and change it as they may choose. Through an intuitive journey, he encourages people to go deep within and thus fine-tune their life's path. I frequently warn people to be careful what they ask for, since they just might get it. Keith remembers thinking, "I don't want to see anymore truth," and soon afterwards, for no medical reason, Keith lost his sight.

When Shakespeare said, "To thine ownself be true," no one could better testify to the consequences of our disobedience to that command than Keith. He shared his experience of losing his eyesight due to "abused eyes" while filming an environmental, anti-pollution documentary on the Pittsburgh steel mills where the response from guards was to shoot real bullets over their heads. He saw corruption in government, in the corporate world, and in the university he had attended where professors faked research. In his search for truth and innocence, even his experiences in Europe were a disappointment. In the body's attempt to protect him from a psychological overload of exposure to corruption, Keith had awakened one morning with his eyes swollen shut and was suddenly without sight. As a photographer, being blind was like a death sentence and Keith remembers just wanting to die rather than living without his sight. He surrendered to his limitation when he redirected his course and was guided into music. He felt restored hope in knowing that making music would return meaning to his life.

Keith reports the presence of a visitor, St. Germain, who assisted him in assessing how he thought and lived his life. By getting in touch with his higher self, he redirected his life's course, and in three days his sight slowly returned with full vision regained two weeks later. None of the best eye clinics in the country could help Keith because they could never identify a physical cause for his blindness—probably because there was none. The mind is a powerful force and when we are not in sync with our soul's code and purpose, it has a way of reminding us who we are and where we need to go. Our body speaks to us and if we don't listen, it can get really nasty.

As a healer, Keith helped his brother recover from terminal cancer. His brother was skeptical of alternative or complementary medicine, but when down to his last days with nothing to lose, he called upon Keith to help. I suggest you not wait to the very end before exploring the powers of the healing mind and prayer.

Retirement Must Not Interfere with One's Work

Since not one of over a hundred people interviewed were raving fans of retirement, Keith's father's unexpected death may confirm the woes of retirement. As a lawyer and politician who lived with the stressors of a world filled with hypocrisy, his mother insisted that he retire and that they move to Arizona where he could take it easy. After living as a retiree for six months it appears he chose to die rather than live a life without purpose. The family recalls that he put his stamp and coin collections together, got his stocks and bonds in order, and then lay down on his bed to die. I am sure we all have experienced similar situations where it seemed like a friend or relative tidied their life's possessions and finished their business matters to leave their house in order before their departure, whether consciously knowing or subconsciously guided. Ben Franklin commented, "There is nothing wrong with retirement unless it interferes with one's work."

Keith empowers others to be more self-sufficient by not giving them answers which enables and also robs them of their power. He emphasizes that love must be freely given and unconditional to be real love and that "free will" must be free. He provides a safe space for people to witness and confront their own scary and embarrassing truths while exploring different aspects of being human.

Although non-judgmental, Keith does not tolerate people who cop out and shirk their responsibility under the guise of becoming more spiritual. An example of such a self-defeating bluff may be Ricky Williams, the former NFL football player for the Miami Dolphins who ignored his eight million dollar contract and commitment when he left to "find himself" in Jamaica. His professed Buddhist philosophy may serve as a cover-up for a drug addiction, unless marijuana paves the paths to enlightenment. However, Ricky has mentioned having a passion for shopping and photography, which is certainly not the same skill set of a competitive football player. He may be an example of the unhappiness and misery people experience when they are not true to themselves. Drugs often become the unhealthy alternative as we attempt to heal ourselves from the emotional pain of not being in sync. My suggestion is that you do not become a slave to work you don't love even if you're good at it and it pays well

A Loving Heart and a Free Spirit

His definition of a champion mindset is to love and express love more and better to people and the planet. Obviously Keith's most progressive concept of winning is global, expansive, selfless, and based on a loving heart and free spirit. He shared his favorite quote which is from Rumi: "Beyond the ideas of right and wrong there is a field—meet me there." A loving heart and the compassion Keith encourages is well illustrated in the following story:

We all are familiar with the *Serenity Prayer* that so succinctly positions us to optimize the use of our energy. *The Praying Hands,* a picture often associated with the *Serenity Prayer,* is a result of a most compassionate story.   Two brothers in a family of eighteen children were aspiring artists but knew there was not money to attend the art academy in Nuremburg. They flipped a coin and the loser would agree to work in the mines to support the winning brother's art education. Upon completion, the skills of the accomplished artist would then cover the costs for the second brother to attend the academy and achieve his dreams.

However, as for all of us, things are not always as we had planned. Albert lost the toss and thus went down into the dangerous mines to support his brother Albrecht's education. Earning considerable commissions, Albrecht announced at his graduation party that he would now support his brother's dream to also be an artist. With tears streaming and audible sobbing, Albert stood up and said, "No…no…no…no. No, brother, I cannot go to Nuremburg. It is too late for me. Look what four years in the mines have done to my hands! The bones in every finger have been smashed at least once, and lately I have been suffering from arthritis so badly…I cannot even hold a glass to return your toast…. No brother…for me it is too late."

To pay homage to Albert for all that he had sacrificed, Albrecht Durer painstakingly drew his brother's abused hands with palms together and fingers stretched skyward. The world renamed his tribute of love from simply *"Hands"* to *"The Praying Hands,"* which will always be a reminder that no one ever makes it alone.

Earn Thy Neighbor's Love

The late Dr. Hans Selye, the "father of stress," certainly agreed that no one ever make it alone. Winning is determined by how we deal with stress and manage our energies. Dr. Selye defined stress as follows: "Stress is the body's non-specific response to any demand placed on it, whether that demand is pleasant or not." As Selye was constantly asked to shorten the description of his research, he finally got it down to this summary. "Fight for your highest attainable aim: but never put resistance in vain." I think his definition could also serve as a practical application for winning at whatever you wish to conquer and overcome. It's all about energy and creatively moving forward with our personal resources and strengths.

Selye's suggestions for handling stress also apply to winning in life:

1. Find a purpose in life that fits your own personal stress level. In other words, people who are successful are true to themselves and again live out their calling or soul's code. If you are happy in your life's work, you've found it!

2. Control your emotional level by recognizing situations as being either life threatening or non-life threatening. Respond rather than react. Basically we have three choices to every event that confronts us. We can act, adapt, or react. While adapting can be a healthy and positive response, it can also be a passive concession leading to a state of powerlessness and helplessness. For example, adapting to a relationship where there is physical or verbal abuse is obviously not healthy adaptation. However, rather than reacting with an instinctual fight-flight response, taking action and positive steps to permanent resolution results in healthy change and conserves one's energies for more creative, productive activities. In all the Olympians, CEOs, and champions I had interviewed, all of them focused not only on time management, but also energy management, which is far more important for when you're sick or with ill-health, you may have all the time in the world, but no available energy to move in the direction of your dreams. Like money, winners seem very astutely conscious of the fact that they only have so much time and energy and thus choose to spend it wisely.

3. Collect the goodwill and appreciation of others. In fact, Selye suggested that we "hoard goodwill and your house will be a storehouse of happiness." He continually encouraged people: "Love they neighbor as thyself and earn thy neighbor's love." The absence of hate and the presence of love seem to inspire the right kind of energy or "eustress" required to create a positive mindset and to gain the support of others in our efforts to excel. It truly takes a village, a team, and the support of others to go over the top. The synergy and symbiotic

relationships of winners is quite pronounced. Tiger Woods always recognizes the encouragement of his father as the key factor in owning the greens and Liberace attributes his success on the piano to his mother's undying support. The Clinton's seem to acknowledge each other and certainly Ronald Reagan saw his wife, Nancy, as his guiding light. Most athletes give full credit to their coach, to God, or a Supreme Being. None of us are champions alone, at least not for a long while. Sustained peak performance requires undying faith and belief, but also continued support, love, and belief from others, which was so well said by Emerson. "The glory of friendship is not in the outstretched hand, not the kindly smile nor the joy of companionship; it is the spiritual inspiration that comes to one when he discovers that someone else believes in him and is willing to trust him."

Integrity: Doing the Right Thing

There is no integrity without trust which unfortunately can be abused. Since not all champions climb mountains, coach teams, or run big corporations, it seemed appropriate to include a current social change agent, Dr. Jeffrey Wigand, who had the guts to blow the whistle on the tobacco industry, and on his own employer, Brown &Williamson. Dr. Wigand chose to relinquish a very well paying job of almost $400,000 a year to a current income of $60,000 when he chose to do the right thing. Ethics can be a costly choice but one that brings a greater level of contentment and inner peace. Your mattress may not be lined in gold, but you do sleep better. In fact, Jeffrey himself confessed, "I have not been this happy in a long time and am comfortable with myself. Everyday I know I have done something that has made a difference for another human being."

Jeffrey confidently stood up to the intimidation and lawsuits filed against him by his billion-dollar employer who even coerced CBS television to edit the scripts for viewing. Money does give you leverage even with the "big boys." Thank you, Jeffrey, for saving so many lives and improving the health of so many not just here but abroad. In fact, Jeffrey contributed to the national smoking average in Canada dropping from 24% down to 17%. His confrontations on the ammonia and other toxicities added to the tobacco leaves caused tobacco companies to now boldly admit that "there is no safe cigarette."

Of course we all know that a picture can be worth a thousand words and that facts and figures create little emotion or impact on people's buying habits. While tobacco companies put out facts and figures on the harmful effects of smoking, not by choice, they still paint billboards with the happy, popular teen couple smoking their brand of coffin nails. The message of course is that if you want to be "in" and popular, attract the opposite sex, which is how we define ourselves at that age, you need to light up. That image far surpasses the impact of harmful, boring facts and figures announced in a dry, dull manner. Trust me, the mind experts on the marketing team at the tobacco companies get paid far better than those capable psychologists at the Johns Hopkins Medical Center.

His revelation of facts such as 440,000 Americans die each year from tobacco use has helped create smoke-free states such as New York, Delaware, Maine, Florida, Connecticut and others. Ireland is the first country to become a smoke-free nation and will hopefully be a model for other countries where smoking is still somewhat unchallenged. Hats off to Jeffrey, whose courage and moral evaluation prompted him to simply do the right thing.

While winners are always perfecting their game, more than doing it right, they are concerned about doing the right thing. They have integrity. If they win the race on steroids, they have betrayed the spirit of the Olympics and are not champions, but hypocrites.

Getting Fired: A New Beginning

Another situation of ethics being key to a winning mindset is the story of Natural Ovens, a nutritionally-based bakery in Manitowoc, Wisconsin. It was founded by Paul Stitts, a bio-chemist, and now is cooperatively owned with his wife, Dr. Barbara Stitts, a nutritionist. When Paul was asked to take the nutrition and fiber out of foods and then add appetite stimulants, he was in moral conflict and confronted his boss, the president of Quaker Oats. There was also research indicating that puffed products such as puffed wheat was killing the test animals, but as long as the uninformed public continued to buy the harmful product, there were no intentions of removing it from the shelves of the local super market. Profit is king in most industries. To solve their "Paul problem," they simply fired him and blackballed him as well. Winners confront the truth and often pay a price. For some, such as Martin Luther King, Jr. and many others whose foresight made them martyrs, they paid with their own blood.

After doing research on his own for a couple years, Paul bought out a small family bakery with five employees and three broken-down delivery trucks. Paul and Barbara have grown Natural Ovens to 325 employees with one hundred spanking new delivery trucks plus a half dozen semi-trucks delivering their nourishing products to eight states and shipping all over the world. When Harvey McKay talks about the blessings of being fired in his most recent book, *We Got Fired,* Paul is a prime example of how we can create dreams from disaster.

Stop Striving and Start Thriving

Just as disasters can turn to dreams, our triumphs can create trials and tribulations. After reviewing my notes from numerous interviews with so many great minds, I wanted to present you with not a recipe for success, for success is personal and individual, but an awareness of myths as well as consistent patterns. One of my favorite thinkers, Dr. Paul Pearsall, includes thoughts of Matt Biondi, an Olympic Gold Medalist, in his book, *Toxic Success – How to Stop Striving and Start Thriving.*

> *I was never unhappier than the moment when I finally attained the level of success I had devoted my life to achieve. I had become only the second swimmer in history to win seven medals in one Olympiad. I had earned a total of eleven medals in three Olympiads, and a total of eight Gold Medals overall. Yet I noticed that each time another Olympic medal was draped around my neck, a strange thought flashed through my mind: that success as I had thought of it all my life was an illusion…. I didn't want to be heroic-I wanted to show my ordinary needs like anyone else. I wanted to be free to share in a meaningful life with people I loved, to relish the feeling of being a good brother, a loving son, and someday a husband and father soothing my own children and sharing all the wonderfully ordinary chaos of life with someone who loved me not because of, but despite, my success.*
>
> *In my new role as an Olympic hero my life became more complicated, confusing, and less my own. Like most people in our modern culture, I had*

believed that striving to achieve the highest level of personal success would change everything in my life for the better. I had sought success because, like many, I assumed it would somehow elevate me above all others, and that I would feel on top of the world. But with the success I craved came the realization that being on top of the world made me feel less a part of the real world-instead, I felt lost within it.

I had assumed that success would make me somehow immune to daily stress. In fact, my constant striving did not result in any sense of thriving. I had assumed success would give me the freedom to enjoy a life of privilege and prestige. Instead, success enslaved me, because once I seemed to have it, it ended up having me.

Dr Pearsall warns that none of us will ever feel that we have finally arrived because life is a process, not a result. "Life is a journey and not a destination" may be a cliché, but I have found it to be true nevertheless. As Dr. Pearsall points out, if success happens to you because of your full joyful engagement in an activity that causes you to feel content, calm, and connected even as you work hard, you will experience and share sweet success.

Hopefully the experiences of Matt Biondi do not discourage you, but rather enlighten you with a more expanded awareness of personal success so that you don't find yourself asking the question, "Is that all there is?" If our vision is too narrow, we can become slaves to the freedom we seek as we climb the mountain. For every vision there must be a revision, and we must continually redirect and enjoy life as a delightful balancing act.

Beyond The Mountain

After I've climbed the mountain and reached the top, I look down and reminisce the struggle—the encounters, the drives, and that great sense of achievement in saying "I've made it."

I look where I've been and look where I've arrived and question myself with "What next?" Life still is—and I still am—but the top has been reached.

There is only me and the universe which is intangible, difficult to define, grab on to, or hold. But I need something; something out there or something in me, for the mountain I possess, but the universe never becomes ours. It does not support or hold us as the mountain does, but it does provide a mystical experience, an enlightenment which can only be from the top of the mountain when the struggle is over, and one is free to experience that which is.

In the climb one does not have time nor energy for introspection and reflection, for in climbing we look upward and outward. But, when all that lies ahead is behind us, our vision becomes introverted and we discover the pleasure, excitement, and contentment which is ours – both a sense of peace and power which is within each of us waiting to be explored. The spiritual communion of becoming one with the universe, with ourselves, and with each other is an elation and enlightenment beyond thoughts, words, or comprehension. It is a reality of the senses, the feelings, and the higher powers which be. It can only be experienced to be known and understood. It is continually evolving, becoming, and changing, and thus does not repeat itself.

Each moment is a unique, spontaneous, and new creation. Each moment *is*—you *are*—and I *am*—together we exist, live, experience... ***beyond the mountain.***

Edie Raether

CHAPTER TEN

BUSTING BARRIERS: BEATING THE ODDS

*"The difference between a successful person and others is not
a lack of strength, not a lack of knowledge,
but rather in a lack of will."*
Vince Lombardi

Although you may not be a champion, how you deal with adversity can still make you a winner. Realizing life offers no dress rehearsals, those I interviewed were very conscious and covetous of their time, energy, and money, which is essentially a reflection of our time and energy.

In fact, in my interview with Somers White, he mentioned the exact amount of time we were on the phone, down to the minute. He was not complaining, just simply aware of how much time he had invested in our interview. It is not a matter of being neurotic or anxious, but a matter of consciousness and awareness. If you value yourself, you will also value your time and energy, and you certainly don't just do things to "kill time." The other obvious pattern was that they maintained an objective perspective about wins and losses, recognizing that a percentage of the time they would lose or be wrong. They thus would not take it personally or feel failure or defeat. They saw unexpected outcomes as another lesson to be learned, knowing that they were now closer to getting it right.

The Library: Low Cost Mentoring and Coaching

Ruben Gonzalez was willing to do whatever it would take, with integrity, to be a competitor at the Olympics. Ruben, the author of *The Courage to Succeed,* shared how he escaped into high adventure books because of continually getting picked on by kids after moving from

Argentina to New York City at age 6. Although he knew no English, he did know that he wanted his life to be like the adventure books he read daily.

He vividly recalled seeing the summer Olympics in 1972, and at age 10 he decided he would make his way to the Olympics—and not as a spectator. Ruben could not run fast or jump high and was usually the last one picked in gym class. He was not given the gift, nor did he really believe in himself, but he did have the dream and replaced his fictional adventures with those of real-life heroes, including Olympians. Obviously, Ruben had begun to identify with healthy role models and in a virtual sense received some low-cost mentoring and coaching through the public library. Interestingly, the spirit of the event drew Ruben to the Olympics rather than a true interest in athletics.

Victory Is Available for Those Who Pay the Price

Another decision Ruben made at age 12 was to never quit anything he really wanted to achieve, realizing that victory was available to those who choose to pay the price and persevere. He was also given good instructions from his Dad, who reminded him that the books you read and the people with whom you associate determine success. His father added he should not hang out with people over whom he had power and influence (our comfort zone), but rather people whom he respected and had accomplished that to which he aspired.

So many times we are hesitant to ask and seek the mentoring we need, but I would agree with the elder Gonzalez who told Ruben that if you respect a mentor's time and do what they suggest, they love to share their experiences and wisdom. Teachers love good students. Mentors also give us permission to believe in ourselves and convince us that we can do it too. Reading this book is providing you with powerful mentors who hopefully will give you the courage to say, "I can do that!" When Ruben saw Scott Hamilton, another little guy, skate at the 1984 Olympics in Sarajevo, Yugoslavia, he knew that despite his own physical limitations there could be a sport for him to participate. Ahhh, the power of a decision. This approach gave Ruben the well-deserved nickname of "Bull Dog."

Ruben realized he that must have a sport that would be compatible with his structural abilities. After averaging only five minutes of playing time per game over three years, he knew soccer would not be his ticket to the Olympics, just as Shaquille O'Neal, a 7'1", 325- pound center with the Miami Heat would never make it as a jockey. However, Ruben's strengths were tenacity and spirit, which are essential for the Olympics. A bit of physical prowess usually helps too. However, success for all of us requires continual assessment of who we are and who we wish to become; what our strengths are and where we want to go. Bingo! When the student is ready, the teacher appears. Ruben discovered the luge as his calling. The luge is the Olympic sport where you lay on your back on a four-foot sled going down a bobcat track up to eighty mph hoping your helmet protects you. Ruben calls it a waterslide on steroids.

Possibilities Are There – You Create the Opportunity

Ruben, Grandma Moses, and my mother never feel it's too late. When he set out to learn the luge, he was politely told by the training center in Lake Placid, New York, that he was about ten years too late, but when you have a dream, "no" is not an acceptable answer. Knowing that where there is a will, there always is a way, Ruben finally got through the Pearly Gates by representing his home country, Argentina. Yes, when God closes a door, He opens a window, but we have to climb through. In my conversation with Ruben, he emphasized the importance of noticing more, for then we see more, and in seeing more, we become aware of more options and opportunities. Possibilities are always there, but we may need to create the opportunity.

Ruben's opportunities were in Calgary, Canada, 1998; Albertsville, France, 1992; and Salt Lake City in 2002 where he placed in the top 50 in all three, despite being almost twice the age of much of his competition. He was often presumed to be a coach, not a player. Next time Ruben may be three times the age of others. The emotionally charged atmosphere of being among so many great spirits is a bit intoxicating, and for Ruben, the luge is simply a means to his childhood dream and decision to experience the Olympics. Have you aborted your dream due to being lured by dollars or allowing your circumstances to dictate your reality? Do you believe in yourself? Will you creatively seek other options and alternatives? Are you willing to do whatever it takes for as long as it takes?

Olympic participation is expensive, and Ruben's debt increased when he left a secure sales job, although without high rewards, to launch his speaking career that put him on food stamps for a few months. Once again Ruben has risen above, and this year his income was triple that of his best year selling copiers. Very simply, Ruben was an ordinary kid with an extraordinary dream.

Be Bigger Than Your Problem

Ruben needs to have a cup of coffee with another Texan Manny Diotte, who overcame the odds and is the author of *Happiness is a Pair of Shorts*. Diagnosed with Hodgkin's disease at age 6, Manny confirms that it was his adversity that gave him the drive to overcome and succeed. He feels this drive is stronger in some than in others because of a mindset or how one programs his mind. His attitude has always been that he is bigger than any problem, which he transforms into a positive outcome. At age 35, Manny has had one or two surgeries every year since age 6, and in spite of almost four years of total hospital time, in 1987 Manny became the youngest realtor in the country. You won't find him in the bleachers.

Severely depressed and just wanting to die, Manny recalled when at age 18 he was driving 120 mph hoping to crash and end the pain, but his faith converted his tragedy into something fruitful and he now refers to the cancer that almost took his life at age 7 a blessing. He now inspires audiences and provides hope to others, emphasizing the power of language in how we speak to ourselves and to others, for words can both hurt and heal. Choose your words wisely.

Sometimes Winning Is Not Being First, but Just Finishing

Manny also urges people to take inventory and reflect so we are not just aimlessly existing but really living our purpose and vision. He does not define winning as being first. For many it may be just finishing: giving it everything you got and doing your very best. With a strong belief in God, Manny is committed to leaving the world a better place than he found it by giving love and sharing knowledge. Together we can make a difference—one heart, one soul, one person at a time. Making reference to Zig Ziglar's comment on not giving up until you're taken up, Manny states, "To rest is to rest."

When Dr. Rosemarie Rossetti, author of *Take Back Your Life*, was hit by a three-ton tree laced with electrical wires while celebrating her wedding anniversary with a leisurely bike ride, aspirations had to be altered. Becoming paralyzed, she had not only lost her independence and mobility, she lost all desire to live until she shifted her thinking and found new meaning in the art of loving and, like Manny, gained a sense of control by choosing her attitude.

From Despair to Triumph

Another independent man with spunk and an undefeatable attitude is the classical music composer, Ludwig van Beethoven, born in Bonn, Germany, in 1770. The powerful driving force of his music stirs my soul, empowers me, and calms me all at the same time. Now, I am not sure how that neurologically can be accomplished, but some things are best simply enjoyed and not analyzed.

Beethoven's dynamic life of despair and triumph is so well expressed in the music he composed, but it is also a reflection of the essence and thinking of all winners and champions. Young Ludwig's father subjected him to a brutal regimen, hoping to exploit him as a child prodigy. Abusive intentions such as stealing the spirit of another human being never win in the big picture, and his father's efforts to control his son's destiny failed.

Fortunately, teachers and members of the local aristocracy recognized his genius and nurtured his innate abilities. He moved to Vienna, the center of the music world at that time, and surrounded himself with magical mentors such as Mozart, who was most impressed, and Hayden, who invited him to become his student. However, Beethoven's unorthodox musical ideas offended the old master, and he terminated his lessons. It is the price we pay when we color outside the lines, as author Jeff Tobe writes about in his book, *Coloring Outside the Lines*. Beethoven may have been the inspiration for another book by Jim Collins, *First Break All the Rules*.

Beethoven studied with several other eminent teachers, but he was developing according to his own singular genius and could no longer profit greatly from instruction. We all need to march to our own drummer and walk on unbeaten paths to create a future that is not just a repeat of the past. If we all would only do what has already been done, we would still all be walking to work (which certainly might have some health benefits but it would certainly extend your one-hour commute). Being controversial is a good sign of creativity and breakthrough thinking. Most people hug their patterns of the past and resist the change that threatens them with a fear of the unknown.

Obstacles Increase Commitment and Conviction

The greatest obstacle in Beethoven's life was being totally deaf. This is probably the worst limitation for a music composer, but our passion and desire to fulfill not only our dream but also our destiny will not accept excuses or exceptions. The obstacles in our lives are there for us to become more creative and committed and thus stronger in our desire to triumph.

As a pianist he had fire, brilliance, and fantasy as well as a depth of feeling. His obvious innovations in style and emotional content expressed freedom, justice, and heroism. Life lacks luster without these qualities, and without a fire in our belly there can be no burning desire to produce the eternal flame. Because of Ludwig's uncompromising ways, no woman ever matched his ideals, and thus he never fulfilled his wish for married love. Although he did fall in love several times, they often were with women who were aristocratic pupils, usually married and thus unavailable. He thrived on challenge, even in his personal life. Actually, his boorish ways and temperament, being a bit eccentric with episodes of rage, may have made his music more appealing than his qualities as a life partner. Perfection may offer greater reward in musical composition.

The theme of never giving up or quitting was illustrated by Beethoven when *Fidelio* had a very unsuccessful premiere. It was then revised, not once but twice, until they finally got it right and savored the victory of a job well done in 1814. That was also the year of the great disaster in a charity performance due to his deafness, which had now taken him into the depths of despair and depression. It is difficult to be productive when depressed, which was only made worse by anxieties and legal actions regarding the custodianship of the son of this late brother. Life happens... to winners as well, but they always seem to bounce back by rekindling the human spirit to once again overcome the obstacles by rising above.

Out of Beethoven's dark night of the soul came his most profound and triumphant music which reflected his victory over his fate. He broke all the rules to create a new plane of spiritual depth with exalted ideas, abrupt contrast, and emotional intensity. In his *Ode to Joy*, you cannot possibly just listen to the music without feeling his struggle and agonizing efforts transforming into profound victory and triumph. You can't keep a great man (or woman) down until they're down. In

1827, he was laid to rest at a funeral that drew over 10,000 when conventional travel was by foot.

There is no failure, but only feedback. Life is a series of lessons to be learned. What lessons are you learning? What revisions are you making to your life's script and what role will you play in the final revision of your drama or performance? (Remember, no matter how great you are or how much you have accomplished, the size of your funeral will still depend on the weather.) Do it for you!

Find a Job You Really Love
Your Life May Go into Overtime

Speaking of overtime, it was recently reported that Irene Newman from Madison, Wisconsin, died at the age of 109. She was a graduate of my beloved alma mater, the University of Wisconsin, in 1917, before women had the right to vote. But once she could, she racked up votes for 22 consecutive presidents. Her college diploma cost her ten dollars, which probably was a good investment since she actively used it for over fifty years and never stopped learning. Asked what the secret was to her longevity, she simply replied, "Find a job you really love because life is too short to do something you don't like." Remember, at 109, *your* life may be even shorter.

Winners think young even when the numbers disagree. Lillian Wright, an 84 year-old woman in the Temple University Hall of Fame, teaches the elderly (many years her junior) sports and still is a frequent referee. She has no intentions of retiring from sports anytime soon and confesses that she was late for her own wedding, a marriage of almost 62 years, because she had coached a game earlier that day. (I am guessing it went into overtime!) Lillian is a woman who knows her priorities.

Optimists Believe They Have Control
Even When They Don't

Whether it was a coach, mentor, teacher, or even a referee, winners report that there was someone who believed in them, validated them, and gave them permission to succeed. Dusty fondly remembers his third grade teacher, Mrs. Rogers, who was a primary influence simply because of the way she made him feel. While we often forget what people say, and sometimes we forget what they do, we never forget how they made us feel.

Leslie Charles, author of *Why is Everyone So Cranky* and *All is Not Lost,* says her kindergarten teacher loved her and saw her potential by affirming, "You can do anything you want to if you put your mind to it." Those words seemed to plant seeds that eventually blossomed. Leslie created her own mountains that she eventually conquered. With no self-esteem and no dreams, big or small, at age 16, Leslie found herself in a less than desirable marriage and with child. With a 10th grade education, no skills, and thus terrified to be on her own, Leslie soon had three children but no child support. Having no car, she hitch-hiked to work which was a legitimate means of transportation back in those days.

Leslie said she learned three important lessons when she began to ask questions, although she was reprimanded for being a curious child. When we ask questions our brain automatically searches for the right answers that guide us to where we need to go. Leslie took responsibility for her desperate existence and once she learned she could learn, Leslie spread her wings and has never stopped flying. Hope causes people to weave sticks that build cathedrals that take a lifetime. Optimists believe they have control even when they don't.

Assume Your Success

Always hopeful, Hope Mihalap, author of *Where There's Hope—There's Life,* found her passion in simply making people laugh and feels her humor won her all kinds of prizes she really didn't want. She never had high goals or a strong desire to win or accomplish great things. Her humor made her popular and thus was elected into all kinds of leadership positions in college. In fact, she recalls being in a study on how leaders think and threw off the theory. However, winners think independently.

Although Hope did not consciously plan her success or have specific goals or ambitions, there were influencing factors—as there always are. She did mention that her father had great wit and as a public speaker would mesmerize people telling stories. Hope simply did what was fun and what she enjoyed doing most, but always did her best. Doing what comes naturally brings us to our unique gifts, which for Hope is making people laugh and making them happy.

Hope also mentioned she just assumed she would be funny and people would love her. I can't emphasize enough the power of positive expectations, for they position us for success and attract the supporting efforts needed internally and externally to make it happen. And the more we experience success, the more we will automatically expect it. Winners expect to win in advance. Life is a self-fulfilling prophecy.

Although she didn't think big, she eased into roles where she did big things. After all, action is what counts, and Hope did have the confidence to reach out and just do whatever was needed to have fun. Since her father's prediction of just getting married did not pan out, Hope needed a job and loved opera so she called Boris Goldovski of the Boston Conservatory of Music at his home. Goldovski hired Hope immediately after professing to being a star typist at ten words per minute. Many times humor and the bond it creates has more value than one's skills. Although she met none of the qualifications for the clerical position at the Metropolitan Opera in New York City, she got the job! Obviously, this was before rules on age discrimination, as she was told right out that she simply was too young. As Rudolph Bing's secretary, she remembers at age 22 conducting the Pittsburgh Symphony, but like most of her life, she is not sure how that happened either.

Although seeming rather random in her successes, I searched to find rhyme and reason to Hope's wonderful mishaps, not to be confused with Mihalap. Hope did try things, just about anything if it did not harm others. There was early role modeling from her father and encouragement from her mother. She always did her best, but most important of all, she connected. People loved her and thus found justification to override her skill deficiencies. Winning is all about relationships, not just in sales and leadership, but in life. Hope also liked to play different roles, which I strongly encourage every parent and grandparent to promote in children at an early age. In a study of highly successful people it was reported that even more than goal setting, the one thing successful people had in common was acting: drama club and high school plays. When we expand our comfort zone to a variety of roles, we connect with more people more of the time and when there is a connection, we make things happen.

Humor creates optimism. Hope revealed that as you exaggerate and describe a bad situation as worse, you hit a breaking point where the humor, like a ray of sunshine, breaks through. Obviously, true tragedies are an exception. Besides humor, Hope restores her optimism in tough times with one simple thought. "This too shall pass."

When in a Deep Hole
Rule Number One Is "Don't Dig"

We all hear the phrase, "change your mind...change your life," but we forget to tell people *how* to change their minds and think like a winner. We encourage people to think positively and change their belief systems without giving them the tools for change or at least an understanding of how the mind works so they can move forward in accomplishing their desired goals.

Eric Plantenberg, president of Freedom Speakers and Trainers, claimed the road to success is paved with struggles that are teachers in disguise. In fact, Eric expressed sincere gratitude to his parents for kicking him out of the house when he was 16 years old. He quickly became accountable for his choices that were lessons not found in any textbook. Wimpy parents do not create winners. Tough love does.

Ari Galper, founder of Unlock the Game, agrees with Eric on the necessity of struggle for strength. He encourages people to ask soulful questions that bypass the conscious mind and connect us with our invisible network, the unconscious mind, for directions on how to move forward on the "right" path.

When Linda Forsythe, founder of *Mentors Magazine*, changed her mind and gave herself permission to succeed, she changed her life. After three divorces, Linda went from broke and homeless to one of the most "connected" women in America today. Although independent, she had a dependent mindset that was getting in the way of eventually developing a company that provides teleseminars worldwide. She simply got sick and tired of being sick and tired. Desperation can be a motivator. She admitted that when you are in hole it really feels like a soft place to fall. When you're in a deep hole, Rule #1 is "Don't dig!"

It Doesn't Matter Where You're From
but Where You're Going

Reggie Cochran, another three-time world champion black belt, feels that martial arts and summer Bible camp gave him the guidance to take the high road. Although he came from white trash, he finds comfort in the words, "It doesn't matter where you're from but where you are going."

He warns against dream smashers and used the analogy of never having to put a lid on a bucket of crabs because if one tries to rise above and get out, the others will tug away and pull the aspiring crab back down. Too often we hang out with people who have the crab mentality.

Even our well intending parents can have crab legs. Dr. Don Cameron, President of Guilford Community College, was encouraged to work in the textile mills and just be happy. Mediocrity was all his parents or even the community knew. Champions draw their strength from within when there are no winds beneath their wings. It is a bit ironical that his own high school English teacher said he would never get into the college of which he is now president. That's beating the odds.

Make a decision, or as Yogi Berra put it, "When you come to a fork in the road…take it." Jim's own words of advice are as parents we need to spend time with our kids and not money. Struggles are also good teachers as they often help us make decisions on what we don't want. After working the third shift at the textile mill, he made a decision – and it was *not* working third shift in the mills.

The Joy Factor: Winners Make Choices Not Sacrifices

Winners make choices rather than sacrifices, for what they give up in honor of their passion is a cherished tradeoff. When I took my granddaughter Amanda to her Russian daycare program, Nina Kurbatskaya, the ambitious and dedicated owner, had converted her entire home to a delightful facility for the children, choosing to make the modest basement her living quarters. It appeared to be a huge sacrifice until I saw her pride and joy as she marched me through every corner of her life – the beautiful daycare facility. A gorgeous master bedroom suite is not the secret to a peaceful sleep. It's not the bed that you sleep upon, but the world that you awaken to that brings us joy.

Perhaps beating the odds requires a new definition of winning and what it means to be a champion. Mitch Axelrod added some very interesting insights stating that we are shifting from a life of paradigms to paradoxes and thus need to learn to live with the uncertainty of opposites and make decisions from a both/and basis. Perhaps we need to stop keeping score and learn to enjoy the game, assuming we are playing on the right field. Mitch made reference to the "joy factor" which may be the fun we have when we choose vs. having to do something. Mitch stated that our culture tends to be risk adverse and that most people have regrets for the things they did not do rather than the things they did do. He encourages all of us to "get in the game," which is an appropriate suggestion from the author of *Play the New Game*.

Life Is a Journey to Be Enjoyed Not Endured

Emphasizing that life is a journey to be lived and enjoyed and not merely endured, Mitch feels there is no perfect life but a series of tradeoffs and that winning is about simply playing the game and taking your swings by stepping up to the plate. Mitch recalled when he had the opportunity to try out for the St. Louis Cardinals but did not make the cut for the professional baseball team.   While his father saw it as a tragedy, he perceived it as a wonderful experience to play the game and give it his best shot.   Winners never lose but rather learn, change, improve, and do a bit better next time around.

Mitch referenced a situation where a developmentally disabled child was allowed to run the bases by the opposing team to give the child the experience of winning even though it caused them to forfeit their victory. However, both teams were united as they all walked off the field feeling like a winner, not by the scoreboard but in the hearts of each and every player. If you play only for your own victory, you live a lonely life. Winners are humble and win only when the team wins. In fact, we have also seen teams in professional sports prove that "team" may be more important than talent and always more rewarding. If sports are to teach us about life, then the win/lose paradigm of the gladiators is also a dinosaur. We need to teach the new game of life that simply is not that simple.

I would have to agree with Mitch's premise that we have become a culture obsessed with winning. Seeing parents fighting with parents at their 6 year-old child's soccer game and players attacking their fans in the NBA makes one wonder why we even call it a "game." It often appears more like warfare and even the coaches need to be reminded of the definition of a coach which is a transportation vehicle to take people where they are to where they want to be…without violence.

Mitch also made reference to the Science of Axiology, a three dimensional model of Value Inversion created by Dr. Robert Hartman, a lawyer in Germany who was nominated for the Nobel Prize in 1973, the year in which he died. It explained how and why good people such as the Germans could become involved in the Holocaust under Hitler's leadership and offers a healthy perspective on winning.

Intrinsic values are the highest and unique to human beings. They include love, compassion, spontaneity, intuition, and honor for humanity. It is unique and distinct, just as the life of each human being is. It thus cannot be measured since there can be no comparisons.

Extrinsic values are based on real world material things and can be created and destroyed, rebuilt, and cloned. The example Mitch gave was when the space shuttle Challenger blew up. Our loss and mourning was not of the ship, which could be rebuilt, but of those unique human beings who could not be.

Better to Serve Than Obey and to Love More Than Serve

Systemic thinking is the lowest of the value triage where we see things as two dimensional such as good or bad, win or lose, and black or white. It is polarized and thus you are either for or against any person, nation, concept, or authority. Religions tend to be systemic in their thinking and thus many wars are fought over a right/wrong ideology or territory. Democracy is also a systemic value, where the system dictates that it is acceptable to kill in the name of freedom. If we kill in war, we get a medal. If we kill in peace, we get the electric chair. The Nazis justified their hideous actions with their ideology, which put the state and obedience to the state above the people. To serve is more valuable than to obey and to love is more valuable than to serve. Mother Teresa was one of the few people who integrated all three values for the common good for she obeyed and served out of love.

There is systemic abuse when we participate on the lower value dimension of polarized thinking and regard authority and obedience to the state more than the people it serves. I think most of us have experienced the ineffectiveness of customer service departments who proudly proclaim their rigid policy that may cause them to lose the future business of a loyal customer. Our thinking can delude us into believing we are a winner or innocent when in fact we are truly criminal in our actions toward humanity. The executives of Enron and other white-collar criminals are examples of delusional thinking that is suddenly corrected by reality – when they get caught. Joseph Goebbels, a Nazi leader, denied he ever killed a single person but referred to himself as a people mover who simply put people on trains. Denial and ideology over humanity is always a dangerous weapon, for we cannot bomb people's beliefs. Winning in the 21st Century may require us to not only think outside the box but to have no boxes. Thinking outside of one box simply puts us inside another bigger box, and we can't solve problems with the same thinking that created it.

Perfection Is a Paradox

Perhaps we need to accept that perfection is a paradox, and that life's journey is a series of paradoxes. There may not be just one perfect partner or purpose, but as we change and circumstances change, we may need to redirect our purpose, such as when we become the caretaker of an ill partner or parent. Our value of another human life can only be comprehended in small doses, which is why we spent hours and days talking about the loss of Reggie White, the former Green Bay Packer player, who died the same day over 175,000 lives were lost in Asia and became nothing more than a statistic in the eyes of the media. In his final comments Mitch suggested that we teach our children and ourselves the ABCs of Values:

> **Attention**—Pay attention to what is going on inside you and around you. As we see more and notice more, we create more opportunities. We also need to pay more attention to our strengths and gifts yet to be unwrapped rather than becoming diverted and continually shifting our attention.

> **Balance**—This is what centers us in the dimension and is the ability to see both sides of a situation. With inattentiveness or over-attentiveness to one or more of the value dimensions we are out of balance in opposite ways.

> **Clarity**—This is our corrective thinking lens and determines how much insight and clear thinking one brings to a dimension of value. It reflects our ability to make better choices with clear vision and conviction and to see our truth.

Mitch's emphasis on the power of attention is well illustrated by the instincts of the Moken tribes, traditional sea gypsies of the Surin Islands in Thailand. They were spared from the ravages of the tsunami because of their astute observation skills. Their awareness of changes in the patterns of the sea, the dolphins swimming to deeper waters, and the cicada bugs becoming silent, alerted them to the impending dangers and thus they found safety by moving to higher ground.

The words *want*, *when*, and *worry* do not even exist in their language, but only words like *give* and *take*. Since they have no concept of time, they are ageless, which confirms Mitch's belief that retirement is another systemic, polarized idea that we work like bees and then enjoy life.

I have always wondered that if you work the first half and play the second half, how do you know when you are halfway there? Beating the odds on that one could be very high risk. Unfortunately Sir Winston Churchill's insights are just as true today: "We stumble over the truth from time to time, but most of us pick ourselves up and hurry off as if nothing ever happened."

Competency Is What We Learn Character Is What We Bring

Someone who has brushed himself off but certainly made things happen is Frank Maguire, author of *You're the Greatest*. Frank is also one of the founding fathers of FedEx (Federal Express), a company that changed the way the world does business. Frank stated that while most people take the Merry-Go-Round, he and the CEO of FedEx, Fred Smith, took the roller coaster. Fred had returned from Viet Nam and couldn't get a job while Frank couldn't hold a job. After being fired from Kentucky Fried Chicken, Fred and Frank got together and drew up some outrageous ideas on a napkin that evolved into one of the world's best companies. Those napkin ideas now provide jobs for over 250,000 employees. Besides "On Time—Every Time," FedEx's priorities are: People—Service—Profit. They shoot high with an objective of 100% customer satisfaction. FedEx follows the suggestion of Albert Einstein. "Strive not to be a success, but rather to be of value."

Before FedEx had a growth of 50% per year, the roller coaster has its dips and the company survived thirty-two months of losing a million dollars a month. Frank admits that although they were losing money—lots of money—they never lost confidence in their belief of what FedEx would become. His formula for success echoes the refrain of all winners. Find your purpose; feel the passion; celebrate the results. Their corporate culture emphasizes sharing: shared vision, shared information, shared responsibility. They validate their employees knowing that employees who feel good about themselves will play it forward to their customers.

Like Southwest Airlines, FedEx hires for attitude and teaches the skills believing that you don't develop unsuccessful employees – you hire them! Frank emphasized that you can teach competency but character is what you bring to the banquet table of life. In his keynotes Frank confirms the power of validation, trust, and caring for it is only with the heart that one can see clearly. With strong spiritual values, Frank claims that success and leadership is a result of the light behind your eyes and asking the right questions.

There is one thing FedEx will not do—promise more than they can deliver. They recognize that relationships and the point of contact with the customer is the strength of the company. FedEx is fearless of the disappointments resulting from extraordinary expectations but dreads the dangers of underachievement. As you transition from fear to faith and from anxiety to attitude (a good one), you become the "producer" of your life. Life is a stage and that there are no dress rehearsals. Franks suggests that you put up a sign—"It's Showtime!"

"Actions speak louder than words" is Frank's mantra for he strongly recommends that we all observe the actions of others more than what they say. The body doesn't lie and you can't stop sweat. In other words, you cannot *not* communicate so be aware of what your silence is saying. There is no place to hide, for hiding communicates a message. Frank cited Ralph Waldo Emerson. "What you do speaks so loudly, I can't hear what you're saying."

CHAPTER ELEVEN

GIVING IT THE BEST YOU'VE GOT: NEVER, NEVER, NEVER QUIT

> *"Nothing in the world can take the place of persistence.*
> *Talent will not; nothing is more common than*
> *unsuccessful men with talent. Genius will not;*
> *unrewarded genius is almost a proverb. Education will not;*
> *the world is full of educated derelicts.*
> *Persistence and determination alone are omnipotent."*
> **Calvin Coolidge**

Although how we start what we set out to do is important, it is how we finish that really matters. Anyone can start a race, but few finish. It is not success but stamina. Perhaps true genius is perseverance in disguise, for it is persistence that makes the impossible possible. What enthusiasm is to ideas, perseverance is to the manifestation of will fueled by a relentless purpose for which many will give of their life.

Starting Over: Again and Again and Again

When it comes to never giving up, I thought of a couple of farm boys back in Green Bay, Wisconsin, who began an insurance company in the living room of Ron Weyer's home. Wisconsin Employers Health Insurance was born of humble beginnings, but that changed when it was purchased by American Express and became Fireman's Fund. Ron Weyers and Wally Hilliard were a dream team that fate seemed to bring together. Ron admitted he was a "C" student due to lack of time to do his homework. His day began with farm chores at 5:30 a.m. and ended with chores at about 8:30 p.m. Being the oldest of seven children, Ron had the first-child syndrome of feeling extremely responsible and that more was expected of him.

He did make the team in the various sports but seemed to only play when it was safe to put in the "B" squad. Enjoying the freedom that cash provided in his summer job driving milk to the cheese factory, young Ron decided not to finish high school but to continue his job earning $50.00 for a week's work. After finishing five years in the military, where he completed his GED, Ron married Colleen, from a small town down the road, and became an independent insurance agent with a great mentor, Ed Schroeder. He then switched from selling life insurance to health insurance, which he found more fun and meaningful in knowing he was really helping people.

In 1970 Ron teamed up with Wally Hilliard who was selling pots and pans, but those pots would soon be collecting gold at the end of a brilliant rainbow. Wally was also a poor farm boy whose father had committed suicide when Wally was just 9 years old. He loved to win, as it gave him some control over a world where he had   very little growing up. A compassionate, generous man who had twelve ideas daily before noon, Ron referred to Wally lovingly as an energizer bunny.

With seventeen employees in a modest home, it was a bit crowded, and in less than two years they built a 10,000 square foot building. Growing pains forced them to once again build another 12,000 square foot building a year later, and again two years later they finally confessed to their success and built an 88,000 square foot building in 1976. Six years later in 1982, American Express, owners of Fireman's Fund, offered a couple of farm boys selling pots and pans 10 million dollars which sure was a lot more money than what they could make milking cows, so they considered themselves rich and accepted the offer without the expense of expert advice, which seemed an unnecessary expense.

Never Sell Yourself Short

Their own image of greatness had not expanded as fast as their company, and they soon realized they had sold themselves short. In 1986, American Express sold Ron and Wally's blood, sweat, and tears for 215 million dollars, which could have bought all the cows in the country. Attempting to rectify their mistake, they attempted to buy back the company, but could not outbid a giant in the industry, Lincoln National Life. Ron admitted that the real fun was in growing the company and making things happen. Since they continued their positions as employees of their own startup company, they still were enjoying the process, just not the profit.

Lincoln National Life had not developed an appreciation for their entrepreneurial spirit and began to stifle the very talent they had purchased. While Lincoln National overall had lost 77 million dollars in their health division, Wally and Ron's group had made one million dollars for them. To really motivate the players who like to win, Lincoln National Life gave a bonus to all other divisions if they lost less than 35 million, but the Green Bay office had to make 15 million for the same bonus. Now, I believe in out of the box thinking but this is simply off the planet and does not qualify as "thinking." Another example of perverted reverse psychology.

Intolerant of the injustice to their beloved employees they confronted the executive team in Fort Wayne, Indiana. While in Fort Wayne getting their pink slips, guards were put in front of their office doors allowing them never to return to the turf and territory upon which they had built their dream and a very profitable company. Power is never an excuse for betrayal.

Ron was 48 and was ready for a small break called retirement but Wally, then 55, wanted to get the adrenalin fix of another charter company so in 1988, just six months after they had been fired from their own company, Wally and Ron created American Medical Security with two desks in an office, but soon were hiring fifty people a week, with 190 of their first 200 employees being from Lincoln National Life. That number increased to 3,000 employees by 1996, when they had sold it to Blue Cross Blue Shield. They had learned from their previous very costly dress rehearsals and this time they played to win and did.

Superstars Are Team Players

I am from the same farm area where Wally and Ron got their start and strongly believe that farmers are the original entrepreneurs. No one survives in farming without a very strong work ethic. Ron and Wally started their days at 5 a.m. in the morning milking cows, squeezed in a school day with sports after and then finished chores at 8 p.m. or later. You learn to manage time without reading a manual on it. Farmers also demonstrate the pride of ownership that motivates everyone to give it their very best shot.

It's all about ownership, for when you build your own company you don't steal from it or the team that took you to the top. Obviously the thieves at Enron did not have the pride of ownership. When you plant the corn, fertilize it, help it grow, and then reap the rewards at harvest time, you understand the entire process from the alpha to the omega. Assembly line learning or management is piece-meal and lacks the depth of understanding, pride, and commitment it takes to make things happen whether it is growing a crop or a multi-million dollar company.

Ron's humbleness, gratitude, and surprise of his own accomplishments were somewhat amusing as he still seems in disbelief that he is no longer on the "B" team and has now earned all the applause of a star player. He reports that the greatest influence in his life is his partner Wally, and his greatest gift is his wife Colleen, as well as his determination and stubbornness. Another gift that I saw is Ron's caring, compassion, authenticity, and sense of fairness with a desire to serve – the company, the employees, and the customers.

Wally and Ron were born to serve by knowing exactly what the customers wanted and needed. They became the first commercial company to do away with claim forms, a procedure that caught fire and now has been adopted by all insurance companies. Their roots as farmers gave them a mindset and skills to never feel defeat. Farmers are constantly challenged by the threats of nature and thus must be innovative problem solvers to survive. Common sense, no longer common, is essential. Quitting is never an option, unless you want skinny kids.

Passion Produces Profits

Garrick Zielinski, founder of Wisconsin Financial Advisors, is another success story of a man with a humble beginning. In a recent visit he informed me that his most competent partner, Nicholas Enea, was buying him out after making a better offer than American Express (who seems to be buying out everyone in Wisconsin). Being one of his original clients back in 1987, I remember my first visit to his fashionably archaic office (an old building where the floors creaked and everything echoes) with modest trappings. He now leaves Mr. Enea with a premiere property. When I warned Garrick of the woes of retiring at age 48, he reassured me that he was eager to start another business as an advisor to divorce lawyers. You guessed it, it's his true passion.

Like Ron Weyers, Garrick had no fancy degrees but rather a strong work ethic that was necessary for survival. There were no free lunches. They both had a keen mind to detect opportunity or create it, and they both identified needs and problems to be solved. A big problem for Garrick was when he was suddenly forced to leave college at 19 to run his father's furniture store. After years and years of hard work designing furniture finishes, Garrick's father at age 47 took the plunge and put every last dime into his life's dream of having his own furniture store. Three days after opening the doors, his father unexpectedly died of a massive heart attack. Garrick, who may have preferred to be at the local pub with his college friends, now found himself running a business he knew nothing about and was soon straddled with a $250,000 debt. As luck would have it, his wife delivered a son prematurely and in heroic attempts to save his son's life, a battle that sadly was lost, he now had an additional medical bill of $50,000. Life happens and it is how we rise to the challenges that makes or breaks us. Although advised by all to file bankruptcy, it was not his character, and in 1988 he finally paid off his very last debt.

We Learn – We Earn – We Return

A graduate of the school of hard knocks, after closing the furniture business, Garrick quickly rose to the fourth highest paid salesman out of 1,600 new recruits in the Harris Company. (You have to stay in the game to win.) Garrick believes that consistency and persistence, along with a strong work ethic, are the key factors to making a difference and confirmed it with the following story:

Other than the lessons from his demanding father, Garrick said his mentor was a short Russian Jew who was an atheist by his claimed skepticism of everyone and everything. Harry Emold made a ton of money with a furniture liquidation company, Unclaimed Freight. Garrick had heard that he had helped another guy out when also deep in debt so Garrick was hopeful that his generosity might be extended one more time. When he paid the cantankerous old man a visit, he was cussed at, sworn at, and basically thrown out of his shop with Emold's screaming voice still echoing in his ears.

Being desperate for help and knowing Emold started his day early, Garrick waited for Emold to arrive at the usual time, 5:00 a.m. sharp. Knowing Emold was his only hope, his begging, pleading, and persistence finally broke through the wall of defense of the defiant old man. Emold not only helped Garrick sell his furniture, he gave him everything he wanted. Don't let "no" ever get in the way of your eventual "yes."

Amused by the idiosyncratic nature of Emold, Garrick recalls sitting in the local pub (one of which Milwaukee has on every corner). A man sitting at the other end of the bar, a stranger to both, muttered that he didn't have a problem that a thousand dollars would not solve. At that point Emold handed the man a thousand dollars and said, "There aren't a million dollars that could solve my problems."

Feeling somewhat guilty about taking the money, the recipient eventually found Emold and insisted on returning the money. Emold refused to accept the money given as it had been given as a gift, but was so impressed with the character and good intentions of the honest man, Emold then hired him as his warehouse manager and taught him how to earn his own money. Give a person a fish and you feed him for a day, but teach a person how to fish and you feed him for a lifetime.

A very wealthy and wise man, old Emold left Garrick with a couple simple truths:

1. Knowledge will be the key to your success.

2. You are never truly successful until you can teach someone else and help others become successful as well.

In other words, we are all here to clone our successes, as another way of paying it forward. We learn—we earn—we return.

Finding Your "Why"

Another man who earns, learns, and returns is John Di Lemme, founder of Find Your Why. John feels we are all born champions, and as miracle makers we all have a unique life print much like our fingerprint. Once you are clear on your "why" and the purpose of your being, nothing is beyond reach. He stressed personal development over education. You can educate a fool, but you can't make him think. Education is too often about stuffing the brain rather than developing the mind.

Labeled a stutterer and misdiagnosed as deaf, doctors confirmed that John would always stutter. He states that we either have a fear or faith mindset, and he emphasized the brain in our heart as our source of power. The acronym he uses is FAITH: Find Answers In The Heart.

He cautions people on getting into a rut or life's grooves and insists that you must take your foot off the brake to fly forward. He also warned that your brakes may be the people with whom you associate. The decision to cut off your past can be a redefining moment allowing you to move forward. A possibility thinker, John referenced President John F. Kennedy who refused the vice presidential nomination and would only run as a presidential nominee because if you choose second place when first is possible, you develop a habit of thinking you're second. Perhaps that is why he suggests we filter our negative thoughts just as we filter the water we drink.

While ninety-five percent of people live life just going through the motions, only five percent actively design their own lives. Our financial blessings for planting a service of value give us the right to receive the reward. If you don't accept that you deserve it, you will probably lose it. Eighty-two percent of lottery winners lose their many millions within twenty-four months. Remember you can't be a blessing unless you're blessed, and the greater your financial blessings, the more you can solve great problems for others. John and his wife sponsor a Christmas for ten impoverished children and I am guessing that number will continue to grow as their blessings do.

The Loudest Applause May Be Silent

A recipient of the Cavett Award, the most cherished award in the National Speakers Association, Rosita Perez has a truly loving spirit and puts a magic spell upon all in her presence. In requesting her to share her thoughts on what is a champion, I received the following letter, which brings the glory of the gold close to one's heart.

Rosita recalled that as a kid, champions were found on cereal boxes or featured at theaters in the Movietone News, magazines, or newspapers. Now approaching the age of 70, Rosita realizes we are surrounded by champions if we simply look around and absorb the spirit of just plain folks who exhibit strengths that many of us forget we have until we most it—and not one moment sooner.

She reminisced about the champions she met twenty seven years ago when as a social worker she inspired her patients with her healing music as she strummed her guitar. She saw the frustrations of quadriplegics and those who could not walk or talk wanting to applaud her but were unable to even swat a fly off their noses. She suggested that they blink their eyes rather than clap their hands. Rosita was changed forever when she saw an audience of bright blinking eyes and states that it was the loudest applause she has ever received in twenty two years as a gifted speaker.

She referred to her mother-in-law who came from Cuba in 1929 with a resume that simply said, "Me works for money," and after 94 years of a fulfilled life said to the priest at her last rites, "I am ready to go home. I have had a good life. I have to rest." That's the humble but happy exit winners have.

Rosita continued in her reflections:

I was asked what motivated me to go from an office job to the main platform of Fortune 500 companies as a keynote speaker. Two words came to mind: fear and desperation. Nothing gets me to change more than those two emotions. Fear that unless I took action I would die with my music in me, and desperation to realize that I was forty years old and had spent my life caring for kids, wiping fingerprints off walls, shopping with three little kids, cooking, and all the time I felt I had something of value to share with the world. I just did not know how to make that happen.

Don't Die with the Music in You: Sing Your Song

The other motivating force was knowing that my dear mother died at age 60 with all her music in her. She was replaced by a machine as a cigar maker, but with so much unrealized talent, I was committed to sing her unsung songs. I remembered the first 'Law of Wingwalking' that advised: 'Never leave hold of what you've got until you have hold of something else.' I decided that did not apply to me. I had to let go completely and instead follow what Ray Bradbury advised: 'We jump off cliffs everyday and we build our wings on the way down.' For too long I had stood on the edge of the cliff waiting to be thinner, smarter, more sophisticated, and it was not until I realized 'I am enough right now' that I was able to transform my life. The success and the money came like manna from heaven once I had committed to the Universe that I would simply be who I am and live my passion for making a difference, knowing being a champion was not a 24/7 endeavor.

In 1989, I was diagnosed with multiple sclerosis, which explained why I stumbled, fell, broke bones, and lacked the energy to hold my arms up to comb my hair. My physical limitations created a forced compromise with my passion for speaking, realizing now that being a champion to one person (my husband, Ray) is simply enough. Like Johnny Carson I chose to stop on top, for being a champion is to know when life is asking us to just step aside rather than receive the hollow sound of 'pity applause' from a polite audience. Maybe that is all love is: not flowers and jewels…just laughter.

Rosita added her favorite quote was from Sir Rabindraneth Tagore, the Nobel Prize winner for literature in 1919. "My songs of life are still unsung. I have spent my life stringing and re-stringing my instrument." Rosita also referenced Carlos Castanedos who had written: "Death is a blackbird perched on our left shoulder and everyday we look at the bird and say, 'I know you're there, but first…'" And we go on and give it all we've got.

It's Always Something

Gilda Radner gave it all she had, knowing the blackbird was perched on her shoulder. In spite of living the success formula, Gilda Radner, the unmatched *Saturday Night Live* comedienne, lost her hard-fought struggle against cancer, but she never allowed her diseased body to destroy her spirit. In her seriously funny autobiography *Gilda Radner – It's Always Something*, she includes one of my favorite Zen parables.

A man traveling across a field encountered a tiger. He fled, the tiger after him. Coming to a precipice, he caught hold of the root of a wild vine and swung himself down over the edge. The tiger sniffed at him from above. Trembling, the man looked down to where, far below, another tiger was waiting to eat him. Only the vine sustained him. Two mice, one white and one black, little by little started to gnaw away the vine. The man saw a suspicious strawberry near him. Grasping the vine with one hand, he plucked the strawberry with the other…. How sweet it tasted!

Although champions live their lives to the fullest, when cancer is ravaging your body that choice is lost.   Gilda struggled with her treatment that forced her to forget days at a time and caused her to miss out on all the fun stuff happening out there. Losing a day on earth was devastating, yet so many spend most of their days just "killing time." While quiet time, meditation, and think time can be productive, creative, or personally rejuvenating, I am still puzzled as to why anyone would choose to kill time.

I Wanted to Only Be What I Am

Winning is about people becoming who they already are and living life on purpose…*your* purpose. Gilda's pleas to live were just that. "I wanted to only be what I am – a comedienne, a jester." Gilda wanted so much to just be funny again, it truly was her calling and in my opinion, *Saturday Night Live* has never been the same since. Gilda may not be just a hard act to follow, but an impossible one to follow. She was willing to do whatever it would take: surgeries, a Port-A-Cath, anything to be funny once again.   She proclaimed it would ignite her spirit to do it. Lighting our spirit may be somewhat like the excitement of the Olympians when the flame is lit at the opening ceremonies. How do you ignite the spirit and the eternal flame or burning desire within your heart that is wanting to become a torch that lightens your way?

Since Gilda died in May of 1989, I obviously was not privileged to have a personal interview, but she admittedly did have regrets. She was bulimic and admits the obsessive eating and throwing up took charge of her life, although her comedy grew from her neurotic way of life. Gilda's priorities were clearly out of whack as she reveals that the most important thing was those 90 minutes live on Saturday night. Even when her whole world was falling apart as long as she could find a joke in it and make up a scene her life was fulfilled. It seemed to create a cloud of denial and for those magical five years she felt immortal.

As Gilda reflected on her past behaviors she realized that we do things "towards life" and things that are "against life." Feeling immortal and deviant, Gilda recalled answering someone who asked her why she smoked with, "At least I have a say in my own death. At least I'm causing it, instead of having it sneak up on me." Having worked with many eating disorders and addictive behaviors, the irony has always been that those who give up control to an addiction disguise the problem as their personal power with a sense of being in charge. Mind games have no winners. However, we can learn from Gilda's experience to do the right thing…*now*, for the laws of cause and effect do not punch in on *your* time clock. Gilda admitted that when she finally caught on and began to change, cancer came along and said, "Remember how you tempted death? Well, here's your opportunity." This was *not* funny.

When Time's Up – Will You Be Pleased with the Trip

While I have always respected Gilda's commitment to excellence in her work, her hope-finding spirit in her fight against cancer drew an even greater love and respect. Like the perfect storm or that one moment in time at the Olympics, life does not always deal us with the hand that we deserve. However, every champion interviewed concurred that more than winning or losing, it's how you play the game, and as long as the game lasts you have to give it your very best shot. Notice I said "play" the game, not watch it as a spectator from the sidelines. The journey of your life was never intended to be a spectator sport. When the game is over and time's up, win or lose, will you be pleased with the trip?

I would like to cite the final page of Gilda's autobiography below, as it so well sums up the essence of how winners think:

I had wanted to wrap this book up in a neat little package about a girl who is a comedienne from Detroit, becomes famous in New York, with all the world coming her way, gets this horrible disease of cancer, is brave and fights it, learning all the skill she needs to get through it, and then, miraculously, things are neatly tied up and she gets well. I wanted to be able to write on the book jacket: 'Her triumph over cancer' or 'She wins the cancer war.' I wanted a perfect ending so I sat down to write the book with the ending in place before there even was an ending. Now I've learned, the hard way, that some poems don't rhyme, and some stories don't have a clear beginning, middle and end. Like my life, this book has ambiguity. Like my life, this book is about not knowing, having to change, taking the moment and making the best of it, without knowing what's going to happen next. Delicious ambiguity, as Joanna said.

When I was little, Dibby's cousin had a dog, just a mutt, and the dog was pregnant. I don't know how long dogs are pregnant, but she was due to have her puppies in about a week. She was out in the yard one day and got in the way of the lawn mower, and her two hind legs got cut off. They rushed her to the vet and he said, 'I can sew her up, or you can put her to sleep if you want, but the puppies are okay. She'll be able to deliver the puppies.'

Dibby's cousin said, 'Keep her alive.' So the vet sewed up her backside and over the next week the dog learned to walk. She didn't spend any time worrying, she just learned to walk by taking two steps in the front and flipping up her backside, and then taking two steps and flipping up her backside again. She gave birth to six little puppies, all in perfect health. She nursed them and then weaned them and when they learned to walk, they all walked like her.

Sometimes Winning Is Merely Surviving

Sometimes we lose even when we don't roll the dice. Sometimes winning is doing the best with what we have and sometimes it is merely surviving, when thriving is not within our reach. My first cousins Don Steinberger and his sisters Mary Ann and Mildred, along with their mother Anna, had to rise to the occasion when John, the children's father, had been accidentally shot by his nephew in a hunting accident at age 44. Don was 12 years old at the time and overnight he had lost his childhood and instantly became the man in the family, filling the empty shoes of his father. He was now expected to run the family farm. His mother was fearful of driving, for back in the forties many women did not venture out behind the wheel. Thus at age 12 Don drove the truck into town to pick up feed and do the necessary errands. Out of compassion and knowing the circumstances, people and police probably just turned their heads rather than turn him in.

Farming requires innovation and strategic problem solving for survival. Don recalled the three-inch blocks that were attached to the clutch and the brake of the tractor so his short legs at age 8 could operate the tractor. Winning is about teamwork where not only all family members but neighbors and relatives contributed as well. When the neighbor's barn burned down, as a child farmer Don was expected to skip school and help rebuild the barn with all the rest of the men. You might call it a benevolent form of social security or a voluntary insurance policy that was probably more effective than our current governmental and corporate systems.

Getting up at 5:00 a.m. in the morning to milk cows, go to school, and then milk again after school until early evening was double duty. I think of so many 12 year-old kids today who can't even remember to take out the garbage let alone fill the silo, make hay, plant the corn, clean the barn, and haul manure, after chopping wood and plowing the fields. This was all while trying to attend school and get a good education. With little time for sports or the Olympics, Don eventually was forced to quit school due to an inflexible principal who would not accept his absence when crops had to be harvested. It's called policies and procedures!

Turning Points: Moments of Truth

Just as Don had a major turning point, so did Donald Driver, a running back for the Green Bay Packers who is a perfect icon of the essence of winners. In an interview with Seth Wickersham of ESPN The Magazine, Donald remembers waking up in the morning as a kid in Houston with a simple but sad question: "Where am I?" Sometimes the answer was a friend's house, other days it was a motel paid for with food stamps, and once it was a U-Haul.

He had nutritious sandwiches of mayonnaise or syrup before wandering out for the night when he would steal cars and deal drugs, although he never used drugs. His mother, Faye Gray, worked the graveyard shift as a hotel security guard, his father became absent after his parents divorced at age 2, and thus young Donald was without supervision until he nearly killed an older woman while racing off in a stolen car. Although he fled the scene, he made a U-turn that turned his life around literally when he went back to see if she was okay. "Sit on my porch," the victim said who also defended him when the cops came claiming that Donald was her grandson. She lovingly confronted him asking, "Why do you do this? You could be doing so much more with your life." That was a moment of rude awakening as Driver realized he hated his life and hated himself for living it. It was a true turning point initiated by a stranger whom he had victimized. Strangers may be mentors in disguise. Embrace them.

Donald and his siblings then left their mother to live with their grandmother who provided stability and structure and thus he traded in selling drugs for sports, lettering in track, football, basketball, and baseball. At Alcorn State he qualified for the 1996 Olympic trials in the high jump. In minicamp in 1999, Driver's idol Brett Favre gave him the affirming nod and said, "Don't worry, Donald, you're going to catch plenty of passes from me." Donald not only catches passes, he also passes his riches on. When not at Lambeau Field catching passes, you can find him in one of several children's charities or one of the local schools creating moments of truth and turning points in the lives of others. Driver's greatest legacy may not be on the football field but the difference he is making in the lives of kids needing a bit of "front porch talk."

Success Is...

To live your life in your own way,
To feel at peace at the end of each day...
To reach for the goals that you have set,
To be proud yet humble when those goals are met,
To be the one that you want to be
While still caring for others lovingly
To know in all matters you've tried your best,
Then you will have found true success.

CHAPTER TWELVE

MAKING A DIFFERENCE: LEAVING A LEGACY

> *"The great use of life is to spend it on*
> *something that will outlast it."*
> **William James**

Paul Arden believes we need to aim even beyond what we are capable of by developing a complete disregard for where your abilities end and simply ask yourself, "How good do you want to be?" Arden says that nearly all rich and powerful people are not notably talented, educated, charming or good-looking. They become rich and powerful by wanting to be rich and powerful.

"The successful man is the one who has lived well, laughed often, and loved a great deal," according to Arthur J. Stanley, philosopher and author. All those interviewed spoke of living up to their full potential by discovering their strengths and natural gifts and then nurturing them to be as fruits on the vine for others to become nourished as well. It was as if they were simply showing up for duty, voluntarily and joyfully. Even one of the most loved presidents in the United States, Abraham Lincoln, admitted, "I am not bound to success, but I am bound to live up to what light I have."

Great Love Produces Great and Everlasting Results

Being a meek woman at heart, Mother Teresa underestimated her contributions to society and the power of love when she humbly said, "We cannot do great things in life; we can only do small things with great love." As evidenced by the impact she had on millions, it is obvious that great love produces great and everlasting results.

In putting it all together and connecting all the dots, some of the conclusion may be a bit surprising. For example, while most of the winners had goals and dreams and most at a very young age, there were others that seemed to stumble on their success and were surprised, even stunned, and in awe of their own accomplishments. Another group had developed their gift or skill and did whatever they loved doing or whatever came naturally as if drawn to their calling by some magnetic force that simply evolved into something bigger than they could have imagined.

Tiger Woods, the first golfer ever to hold all four professional major championships at the same time, is an excellent example of someone who had innate abilities for the game, but was also coached well and encouraged by his father to go beyond. Michael Jordan, five-time NBA most valuable player, was crucial to the Chicago Bulls winning six of eight championships. In fact the two years they did not take it, Michael was out experimenting with baseball. Michael was destined to dribble the ball – not hit it.

The Luck Factor: Preparation + Opportunity

The luck factor seemed apparent for some such as Jack Canfield and Mark Victor Hansen in their brilliant idea to collect and compile inspiring stories and then publish them in a book that has had one of the 82 versions of *Chicken Soup for the Soul* on the bestseller list for over ten years. Now that's an idea! However, what often appears to be luck is really the point when opportunity and preparation come together.

Brilliant and potentially profitable ideas are popping all the time, and for Wally Hilliard it was the daily dozen before noon. Wisdom tells which ones are worth exploring and developing so we don't drain our energies stargazing or engaged in useless pursuits. Once we have chosen the pick of the litter, we need to follow through, persist, and be willing to do whatever it takes without succumbing to perceived failure and rejection. Notice I said "perceived," for most of our obstacles are projections of our own fears and doubts. In other words, we make up most of our obstacles which is a very nasty habit.

If You're Not On Fire... You Can't Light One

The concept of *Chicken Soup for the Soul* would have died an early death of natural causes had Jack and Mark not persisted and kept coming back with new options and entry points. We are so quickly defeated by the frown and sigh of others who don't see the big picture or just don't get it! A lot of success is about being able to persuade and change the way people see things to thus be receptive to your point of view, which is why I had written a book on influence and persuasion. Most successes in the business world and in life are about selling your ideas, your values, beliefs, and enthusiasm. If you're not enthusiastic about what you're doing, you can't light any fires.

As I was rushing to catch a flight, 10,000 copies of my first book were delivered. I grabbed a box to take with me and sold all 44 before I arrived at my destination. Everyone bought one: the teller at the bank, the guy who gave me directions when I got lost, the airline staff, people waiting in line, the security people, and even the skycaps. Some ordered dozens later for gifts. While the value of the book has not diminished, the sales while traveling have dramatically decreased only because it is difficult to recreate the excitement and enthusiasm I had that first day after twenty-seven years of wanting to author a book. We need to celebrate each day as a new beginning and opportunity. Remember, nothing sells like excitement and enthusiasm.

Crucial to winning is not just attaining but sustaining the excitement and enthusiasm our initial experiences with success creates. We must ignite the torch and rekindle the flame again and again and again, even when there is no fire in our bellies. You cannot let your circumstances dictate your emotional state or dampen your passion. Jeffrey Gitomer had clearly differentiated his circumstances from his attitude. "I was broke but I was not down." Winners remain objective and separate themselves from their situations to continually turn obstacles into opportunities. In other words, don't let your circumstances and where you're from dictate where you're going and who you will become.

Optimism Is Turning Obstacles into Opportunities

Optimism may have been the most consistent quality among those interviewed, and was often based on their strong sense of faith and belief in themselves and their futures. They associated their strength, hope, and optimism to their religious beliefs or spirituality. Optimism sometimes is less about hope for the future and more about a gracious acceptance of reality. Ray Charles felt that he only lost 1/99th of what life is about because he was blind, and due to his indomitable will— another consistent quality in winners—he rose above his heroin addiction of seventeen years and became a memorable musician who deserved to have the movie *Ray* filmed in his honor. Ray Charles never compromised his own soul and proudly stated, "I don't sing a song unless I feel it. If the song don't tug at my heart, I pass on it. I have to believe in what I'm doing."

"Don't take your toys inside just because it's raining," claims singer, Cher Bono, who refused to let her circumstances dictate her destiny. Her mother was married eight times and her father was a heroin addict who lived more in jail than out of it. After divorcing Sonny Bono with whom she had a love-hate relationship, she married a drug addict. We often marry people with our parents' problems. Our internal stuff or self-image must match our successes and rewards or we may sabotage our climb to the top. Cher continued, "I'm scared to death of being poor. It's like a fat girl who loses 500 pounds but is always fat inside. I grew up poor and will always feel poor inside. It's my pet paranoia." Cher needs to change her language to free herself from her past.

The more money, fame, and power Halle Berry acquired, the more she suffered from the loneliness at the top. Her father was an alcoholic leaving her with no sense of self and thus Halle seriously contemplated suicide at the height of her career. Halle's love for her mother, not herself, kept her from destroying herself and a world full of possibilities. We cannot act in a manner inconsistent with how we see ourselves. When we don't feel deserving of the glory and love others bestow upon us, the confusion creates a disturbing conflict that we attempt to resolve by destroying the source – ourselves. Rather than destroy the source, learn to recreate it.

Integrity and Compassion: Doing the Right Thing

Dottie Walters, author of *Speak and Grow Rich* and CEO of Walters International Speakers Bureau, recalled words from her Scottish grandfather whenever she fell down and skinned her knees. "It's OK to lie down and bleed a wee bit. However, we Scots never stay down." We all need to lick our wounds to heal, but if we lick them too long we keep the wound open and prevent moving forward. No matter what our nationality, winning comes easier when there is a positive, powerful identity associated with whom we are, even if we have to create it ourselves. Dottie's way of hanging out with people of greatness was to frequent the city library. There she found friends with great minds from whom she could learn and emulate. And the price was right.

Consistency is an essential characteristic in winners. They are consistent in terms of following through with their goals and visions and in manifesting their ideal self-image. They were believable and trusted, which is crucial in all relationships both personal and business, and certainly in parenting, sales, and leadership.

While winners are always perfecting their game, more than doing it right, they are concerned about doing the right thing. They have integrity. Champions come in all sizes, all ages, and all races and creeds. Andrew Gieseler, a 12 year old from Naperville, Illinois, found nine thousand dollars and thought, "Whoever lost this money is going to be in a lot of trouble." Andrew's integrity and compassion for an unknown friend guided him to do the right thing: turn in the money. Andrew also admitted his parents were good role models. By the way, Andrew was well rewarded for his honesty by companies throughout America. It all comes back to us.

Listen! You Will Know What Song to Sing

"If we listen…really listen we will know what song to sing," says Elena Doria, a singer for twenty years at the Metropolitan Opera. She quit the Met to teach young children in the classroom how to sing perfectly, not just their best. "I wanted to do it. I'm not religious, but I think something touched my shoulder and said 'that's what you should do.'"

Whether expectation or divine guidance, Elena's father signed her up for piano lessons the day she was born, but she chose another instrument—her voice. He gave her his simple recipe for success:

1. Sit up straight
2. Pay attention
3. Don't yawn

She took those lessons seriously, for after her studies at Juilliard, she won a Fulbright scholarship to study in Italy. When she made her debut in *La Traviata*, she recalls inhaling a mosquito, but just kept on singing. "It was lovely. Lovely. I loved it." I think this is Elena's way of telling us to not let the little things bug you and bash on regardless.

Keith Varnum confirmed:

Sharing who you really are – and all your natural spiritual abilities – with the world is the ultimate act of love. You can offer others the space to be just as they are. You become capable of giving the greatest gift we can bestow on another being: unconditional love and total acceptance. In the process of 'civilizing' our species, we humans have become conditioned to not feel deep, dynamic passion and love for life…our collective heart has turned to stone. …Life's creative enthusiasm sends us into a panic in the modern sense. Most of us are terrified of living fully alive and free…We humans can re-connect to our natural aliveness by opening to a force that is more powerful than our programming, more compelling than our collective conditioning. The force that can liberate us is universal life energy, primal life force. Fortunately, cultural conditioning cannot control primal life force. This raw creative energy is free and innocent of all human concepts and beliefs. Primal life force doesn't follow its own drumbeat; it is the drumbeat.

Your Unique Plan: The Seed of Knowing Is Within You

In Keith's conversation with Jesus and St.Germain, the following was shared. "Within each of you humans is the failsafe seed of knowing how to undo this particular creation—this creation of being unconscious, of forgetting who you are and why you are here on Earth. Within each of you is the seed of knowing your unique plan and special purpose—your personal contribution to the unfolding of the collective plan. The seed of knowing is within you and when given the right environment at the predetermined time, the seed will sprout and grow."

Oprah Winfrey, actress and TV celebrity, confirmed the seed of knowing is within when she stated, "I knew I was destined for greatness." In spite of living in poverty in rural Mississippi, Oprah recalled that when she saw Sidney Poitier in the movie *Lilly of the Fields*, she said, "I can do that!" When she received the Oscar Award for *Color Purple* in 1985, she quietly screamed, "I did that!" Award-winning actress Whoopie Goldberg, once a welfare mom, humbly confessed to also having a strong intuitive hunch of her greatness. What is your hunch? What action will you take? What are you waiting for?

To give credence to the theory that we all have a soul's code or calling, Neil Armstrong reports that from age 9 he was obsessed with aircraft. Even when younger he had a recurring dream: he could, by holding his breath, hover over the ground. He did not fall or fly, but just hovered. He admits he tried it when awake and it did not work...until his moon mission on July 20, 1969, when Apollo had landed. It truly was, "One small step for man, one giant step for mankind." I see winners as ambassadors of peace and goodwill, whether it is in the Olympic village or the global village. The plaque that Neil Armstrong planted on the moon will hopefully take root for a world beyond the world we know. Reflecting big-picture thinking, that plaque said, "Here men from the planet Earth first set foot on the moon. We came in peace for all mankind." (I remember watching Captain Video on TV when going to the moon and Mars was sheer fantasy.)

Finding the Right Work Is Finding Your Own Soul

When we focus on what we love to do most, we are most authentic and experience a serenity in simply being more of whom we are.   The complexities of life that interfere with our daily joy come not from excessive work or activity, but rather from seeking a truth that is not ours.

Success comes to those who never, never, never quit, but only if the ladder they are climbing is leaning on the right wall. If you're off track, it takes courage and wisdom to quit one activity, job, or relationship for another to free up energy that now can more constructively be redirected toward goals that are in sync with your true calling. Pay attention and listen to your inner voice for gut guidance. Thomas Moore, author of *Care of the Soul,* said, "Finding the right work is like discovering your own soul in the world." Buckminster Fuller, American author and philosopher, agreed, "The minute you begin to do what you really want to do, it's really a different kind of life." When we are manifesting our core genius we feel most alive, renewed energy, calm, content, and joy. All champions interviewed agreed that success is a journey and not a goal. It is a process and not perfection. It is giving it your best shot, with love and integrity, to make a difference in the lives of others.

A Life without Cause Is a Life without Effect

It is not the gold medal and just the one moment in time, but what the medal reflects in terms of our climb to the top. Seneca, a Roman philosopher, said, "One should count each day as a separate life." Champions have winning moments every day, every hour, every minute, and view life as nothing but moments of opportunities. It all begins with a thought. It is how winners think...*differently*. When we connect our thoughts we create our dream.

A dream may be simply a flash of the truth—our truth. We are all dream makers. We are never too old or too young to begin the climb, but at certain times or stages in our lives we may have to alter our choices and choose to climb hills instead of mountains, but we all need to leave trails for those generations yet to begin their walk. When age or disabilities bring limitations to our physical agility, the wisdom we share allows us to give guidance and direction that no map can provide. When our mental faculties may be taken as with President Reagan, may we accept life's stages and embrace that too with undefeatable optimism, which he referred to as the beginning of the twilight years of his life. What is your legacy? What will you leave? Einstein summarized it very well. "A life without cause is a life without effect."

Purpose is life's yellow highlighter which inspires all of us to have an effect. Joseph Campbell sees our search for meaning as a desire to feel more alive. "People say that what we're all seeking is a meaning for life. I say that what we're really seeking is the experience of being alive, so that our life experiences on the purely physical plane will have resonance within our innermost being and reality, so that we can actually feel the rapture of being alive!"

The Human Spirit: Not for Sale

Winning is about freedom and liberating the human spirit. From the Boston Tea Party to carrying the torch at the Olympics, we are all attempting to stretch beyond our physical boundaries and connect with a higher self and experience a spiritual transcendence. As Erik Weihenmayer, the blind man who climbed Mt. Everest said, "It's like you know you're doing something that human beings shouldn't be doing, you know?... I like the spiritual feeling of being on a mountain…no one suffers the way you do on a mountain for a beautiful view. The real beauty of life happens on the side of the mountain, not the top."

People unite when there is a cause or reason with direction and leadership. We saw the same power, heroism, strength, and unity when the World Trade Center was attacked by terrorists on September 11, 2001. Spontaneous leadership and organization was also demonstrated on United Flight 93 when Todd Beamer and the other passengers and flight crew were powerless in their own fate but could save thousands of others by taking action. They focus on what they can do rather than wallow in their limitations, which are often self-imposed. Their actions are often to serve others even before themselves.

Whether it is the Amber Alert, instigated by mourning mothers of victimized children or Mothers Against Drunk Drivers, it is ordinary people doing extraordinary things to make a difference in the lives of millions. Money is never the end goal but merely a means to the end. Money gives them the power to advance their cause and the freedom of choice to direct their energies and resources toward their desired goals of service.

The Golden Rule: Happiness Is Serving Others

"Do unto others as you would have others do unto you" is the cornerstone of every major religion and is also the prominent voice of all those who have lived the good life and made a significant contribution. It is the best lesson in sales, customer service, leadership, and in our personal and family relationships as well. While champions feel lucky and things appear to be by chance, the universe operates according to strict laws. In the material world it is Newton's Law of Motion that declares, "for every action, there is an equal and opposite reaction." From a spiritual perspective it is the Law of Cause and Effect, which makes the Golden Rule more than just a sweet saying.

What you give is what you get. It all returns to you like throwing water against the wind. Every thought you choose molds and modifies your psyche, your character, and your path for good or evil. You are literally doing to yourself what you are doing to others in thought, word, and deed. By establishing a vibrational level with a positive or negative charge, a very focused laser beam goes out and attracts people and circumstances that resonate and are in harmony with you. Your mind is like a broadcasting and receiving station for thought waves of specific vibrational frequencies that you are free to choose, just as you choose your favorite radio station. This explains why Einstein, Gandhi, and so many of the extraordinary thinkers value their intuitive intelligence that tunes into a less obvious but more powerful frequency. As a thinking center, you are able to tap into the pure energy of creative intelligence that is similar to the information highway and is thus the Internet of your soul.

Champions Are Lovers: They Bless That Which They Want

Champions love themselves; they love others; and they love serving. Because they love others more, they give more: of their time, their talents, and of themselves. All of the very busy people interviewed had shared their time, wisdom, and experiences, and had generously given of themselves to make a difference in your life. That is their gift of love to me and to all of you. They love to make a difference in whatever way possible which made the wealth of wisdom and experiences in this book possible.

Winners are also more grateful and as Meister Ekhart requested, "If I can only pray one prayer let it be *Thank You*." It is because they give more, they receive more, and because they are grateful for what they receive, the laws of reciprocity sustain their abundance. There is a Huna philosophy, "Bless that which you want."

Peace on Earth:
Creating a Compassionate Civilization

While you are guaranteed to receive the goodwill that you have given, it may not be from the person to whom you have given it, for the Infinite Intelligence makes that choice. When we as individuals diligently practice the Golden Rule then as nations we will become a compassionate culture and civilization creating true peace on Earth. Champions learn the dance and know that success has more to do with what you do for others than what you accomplish for yourself. Whether it is an artist creating beauty, healing the sick, fixing a flat tire, giving a hug, or hope with a smile, it is as Hans Selye concluded after a lifetime of scientific research on stress, that it's all about altruism and loving thy neighbor as thyself. Getting the gold is practicing the Golden Rule. Winners understand the dynamic exchange and interplay we have with the universe and as we give love we do receive it.

Another example is the senior class of eight from Lima, Wyoming, a town claiming 250 inhabitants on any given day. The classmates had bake sales and car washes since 8th grade and had finally saved over $5,000 for a class trip to the Oregon coast. When they learned that their teacher was diagnosed with breast cancer they cancelled their dream of five years and gave the money to help her instead. Hearing of the story, a fund was then established where they received twice what they had given, and a trip to the coast, however not from the same source to whom they had given. The math works every time but not on a calculator.

Unstoppable:
Your Dreams Must Be Greater Than Your Fears

As we convert the fear factor into future focus, we also convert problems into possibilities. Fears are a result of "what ifs" which are an obsession with the negative, defensive energies that paralyze progress and inhibit creativity, the currency of the future and our survival as a global community.   As we stretch into the unknown territory of imagination and transcend beyond being realistic, which is based on past experience, we become a possibility thinker which compels us to venture out on the limb even without a safety net. Charles Lindbergh flew for twelve hours in total darkness across the Atlantic Ocean. Charles was unstoppable. This doesn't mean that we don't feel fear, but that we just don't let it interfere with desire. What fires burn within you and what might be stopping you from venturing out to the end of the limb and the hanging fruit?

When we have dream, nothing gets in the way; but when we don't have a dream, everything gets in your way. No matter how clear your road to success may be, our dreams must be bigger than the obstacles encountered. When we are truly committed, fears tend to fade as we claim our future.

Action: To Know and Not to Do Is Not to Know

Being a winner is to have mattered and to have made a difference. It may be following my mother's simple instructions: "Leave it better than the way you found it." This includes everything you use and borrow, including the planet Earth. We must all follow our bliss and remain focused, for whatever we think about, focus on, feel, and act on, we attract. The key is to act. There is a Chinese proverb that states, "Man who watches for roast duck to fly into one's mouth, waits a long, long time." We also need to be more focused on the solution rather than the problem which is one of the reasons racecar drivers have their accidents on a curve...they're focused on it.

Winners are bold and have big dreams, but they also sing like there's nobody listening. They don't just go through the motions, but are passionate in their actions. They are not misplaced cheerleaders. Again I refer to Native American Wisdom. "To look is one thing. To see what you look at is another. To understand what you see is a third. To learn from what you understand is still something else. But to act on what you learn is all that really matters!"

Stop on Top: Knowing When to Quit

Winners stop on top. They know when to step down...yes, quit. You've got to know when to hold 'em and when to roll 'em. Tom

Brokaw, the Anchor for NBC, stepped down with high honors. After a thirty-year run earning twenty million dollars a year, Johnny Carson retired from doing *The Tonight Show*. He said, "I think it's a good thing to get out while you're still on top of your game. I found something I always wanted to do and I have enjoyed every single minute of it." Find a job you love and you will never work a day in your life. Johnny said he didn't feel there was anything more he could offer since he had done it all and it was getting harder to top what he had already done. Brett Favre, the Green Bay Packers quarterback, based his decision to continue playing on whether he believed his passes would contribute to the team and put points on the scoreboard. To know when to quit… that is class and true wisdom.

Take Time: Reflect, Pray, Meditate, and Think

The speed at which we live and think may be causing static interference to our ability to get in touch and connect with our wise mind. Winners take time to reflect, pray, and introspect, for almost all emphasized their spiritual or religious life being crucial to their inspiration and success. President Bush admitted it was what has sustained him through some very tough times in this country's history. In discussing the dangers of the increasing dominance of fast thinking, Bristol University professor Guy Glaxton suggests, "My argument is not just that new ways of knowing exist, and are useful. It is that our culture has come to ignore and never value them, to treat them as marginal or merely recreational, and in so doing has foreclosed on areas of our psychological resources that we need." To move ahead faster, we all need to slow down. According to Paul Pearsall we are all too eager to "get to the point." He reminds us that, "Too much 'insight' and not enough 'outsight' can make you appear stupid and slow to the normal world." Daydreaming is not a behavioral problem, for how can the dream come true if you haven't first dreamed the dream?

What Is Your Legacy?

Winners never die—they leave a legacy. Their influence continues because they give it all away. They share more and give not just generously, but endlessly, and thus have impact and make a difference.

They don't keep it to themselves which is probably why many Olympians turn around and inspire the world as motivational speakers. (It also pays the bills.)

In his last days Robert Noel Test expressed the desire we all have to live on when we have passed on:

Living Forever and Leaving a Legacy

The day will come when my body will lie upon a white sheet neatly tucked under four corners of a mattress located in a hospital busily occupied with the living and the dying. At a certain moment a doctor will determine that my brain has ceased to function, and that, for all intents and purposes, my life has stopped. When that happens, do not attempt to instill life into my body by the use of a machine...and don't let this be called my deathbed. Rather, let it be called my bed of life and take my body from it to help others lead fuller lives.

Give my sight to the man who has never seen a sunrise, a baby's face, or love in the eyes of a woman. Give my heart to a person whose own heart has caused nothing but endless days of pain. Give my blood to the teenager who was pulled from the wreckage of his car so that he might live to see his grandchildren play. Give my kidneys to one who depends upon a machine to exist. Take my bones, every muscle, every nerve, every fiber in my body and find a way to make a crippled child walk. Explore every corner of my brain, take my cells if necessary, and let them grow so that someday a speechless boy will shout at the crack of a bat, and a deaf girl will hear the sound of rain against her window. Burn what is left of me and scatter the ashes to the four winds to help the flowers grow.

If you must bury something, let it be my faults, my weaknesses, and all my prejudice against my fellow man. If, by chance, you do wish to remember me, do it with a kind word or deed to someone who needs you.

If you do all that I have asked, I will live forever.

The same thoughts have been expressed by many different authors and poets in different ways. George Burns, an inspiration to all for his entire 100 years, said, "I'd rather be a failure at something I enjoy than a success at something I hate." The reason the song *My Way*, most appropriately sung by Frank Sinatra, brings people to their feet is because he tells it like it is—My Way. Success to me is living life your very own way. It is about overcoming obstacles and seeing opportunities. It is exercising your truth, your freedom, your freewill and choices. It is daring to dream and to dream big. It is perpetually seeing possibilities and creating opportunities knowing that light always overcomes darkness. It is discovering your potential and giving yourself permission to manifest your greatness to live the promise. It is to, as Thoreau suggests, "Go confidently in the direct of your dreams. Live the life you have imagined."

Bash On Regardless!

Winning! is a book of permission. In reading about the experiences of those who have risen above and triumphed, my hope is that it will echo in your heart, "If they can do it...I can do it." Bash on regardless!

It is my conclusion that we are all potential dream makers and dream catchers, although many have programmed themselves to no longer imagine what is possible, which is not what Dr. Phil McGraw means when he says, "Get real." Real is based on past experience and what *is* rather than what will be. Dwell in possibility. We are all mountain climbers in a sense, with some people challenged by The Rockies and bigger mountains than others. Some prefer the mediocrity of the flat lands and still others finds their lives only going downhill or in a perpetual coast mode. It is not about getting the gold, which is simply *a thing* around one's neck and one moment in time. It is more about what the gold represents in terms of perfecting a process and getting a bit better than you had previously been. Also, champions don't have one moment in time, but rather moment after moment with many memories of being victorious, just as Einstein had thought after thought. Winning is a process that begins with the thoughts we choose and the way we think. It is dwelling in possibility. Although concerned about doing it right, there is a greater concern to do the right thing.

Winners dream more and think big, which stirs the soul and ignites their passion to do whatever it takes. Thus, they are more compelled to action, allowing nothing to get in the way of their mission. In that sense they are unstoppable as they exhibit the indomitable will. They value their time and have a high regard for life, not only their own lives but the lives of others. They are notably compassionate and serve others to advance society and improve the world we share. They are leaders and role models and because they simply *care,* they are committed to making a difference. They are eternally optimistic and embrace life as a series of trade-offs and compromises, and the word "defeat" simply is not in their vocabulary, as problems are always perceived as possibilities and obstacles as opportunities. They have an undying faith which for most of those interviewed was based on a strong spiritual sense or religious beliefs which gave them the strength to move forward when the winds were not at their backs.

The most consistent factor was that not one person interviewed had any desire to retire, although some may have stepped aside due to health reasons. Why give it up until you're taken up? People who love to golf don't give it up because they're 65, so why would you allow some irrelevant number in your life stop you from living your dream?

They also had a sense of humor and although they took themselves seriously, they saw life as too precious to waste on worry. Norman Cousins, author of *Anatomy of an Illness,* known to have laughed his way back to health, reminds us all to lighten up! "Laughter is an ambassador to all your good feelings and emotions—love, hope, faith, will to live, playfulness and humor."

These gentle giants were more aware, especially of their blessings, and thus had the attitude of gratitude and saw the glass always full. They had identified their gifts and natural talents and embraced them not only as gifts but as a responsibility, often citing, "To whom much is given, much is expected." We must be accountable more like Frank Bucaro who celebrates every morning as Christmas and every evening as Thanksgiving. In writing this book I have personally been inspired and enlightened by my interviews with those who have shared their insights and experiences. I will be moving forward with a program, *Wings for Wishes,* which is a character building system for children. It will incorporate the lessons in this book to give future generations hope, optimism, and the behavioral tools to manifest their dreams and become winners and champions. Play it forward by sharing the lessons in this book with your children, friends, and colleagues so you too can make a difference. What actions will you take action with the lessons you have learned?

Ralph Waldo Emerson well summed up how winners think—what champions do:

To laugh often and much; to win the respect of intelligent people and the affection of children;

To earn the appreciation of honest critics and endure the betrayal of false friends.

To appreciate beauty; to find the best in others; to leave the world a bit better whether by a healthy child, a garden patch or a redeemed social condition;

To know that even one life has breathed easier because you have lived.

This is to have succeeded.

Abraham Maslow, a psychologist, wrote: "The story of the human race is the story of men and women selling themselves short."

In Maslow's Hierarchy of Needs, he reveals that we all have an inborn drive toward the realization of our full capabilities. That drive to move us onward and upward toward the achievement of our dreams and aspirations can make us feel restless and discontented, and thus we many attempt to numb it with alcohol, drugs, sex, addictions, depression, excessive eating, and a vegetating lifestyle. But it cannot be denied. Embrace it and develop a system of life mastery to move forward with boldness.

Winning is the celebration of life as expressed by Lakota Su:

> *Remember my children*
> *when you were born,*
> *you cried and the world rejoiced;*
> *but live your life so when you die,*
> *the world cries and you rejoice.*

178   Index!

Winning!

Coaching and Retreat Facilitation Programs

The number one recommendation of all winners is to have a coach or mentor. Coaching and mentorship brings clarity to our vision and ignites the passion that propels action. It creates a personal blueprint for your success. In addition to increased awareness and accountability, the *Winning!* coaching programs provide the neuroscientific tools for mastering change and optimal performance.

The Winning Institute Provides Various Coaching Programs: Executive, Individual, and a Group Teleseminar Series

- Creating Your Success Blueprint—Personal Development

- Breakthrough Thinking as a Business Strategy—Professional Excellence

- Sales Success—Powerful Presentation and Persuasion

- LeaderShift—Creating a Compassionate Culture for TeamThink

- Parenting and Family Education—Relationship Enrichment

For more information visit *www.change-strategist.com* or *www.raether.com* and click on coaching. You can also request the information packet by calling (919) 557-7900 or by emailing *info@edieraether.com*.

Winning!

Winning in Business Series

Bring the *Winning!* workshops to your organization, school, or professional association. The workshops and training programs are designed as one and two-day seminars with optional ongoing coaching for sustained peak performance, organizational change, and management development.

For an elevated Return on Intelligence (ROI), learn to implement the "how winners think" principles to achieve personal and corporate alignment for TeamThink, optimal performance, and a compassionate culture. By integrating the neuroscience of achievement with brain-based performance methodologies and incorporating emotional and intuitive intelligence with the Herrmann Brain Dominance Inventory, you will put your company's whole brain to work. Through strategic thinking, inspirational leadership, and innovation as a business strategy, you will maintain a competitive position in the global marketplace.

How Winners Think—A whole-brain model of decision making and problem solving that promotes breakthrough thinking as the currency of the future and innovation as a business strategy.

How Winners Sell—Selling is not selling but buying a piece of the customer's mind. The power of positioning, influence, and persuasion is introduced through buying and selling thinking styles.

How Winners Lead—Inspirational and transformational, the LeaderShift model facilitates change from the "insight" out resulting in the high performance synergy of TeamThink.

How Winners Serve

How Winners Create Wealth

How Winners Celebrate Relationships

How Winners Embrace Health

Winning!

Programs for Children, Adolescents, and Family Development

How Winners Parent

The parenting series redefines the parenting role as one of spiritual guide, developmental mentor, and success coach in addition to the traditional parenting activities. Learn to be a facilitator of your child's soul code and core genius to maximize potential for optimal performance.

Wings for Wishes

Wings for Wishes is an integrative, experiential-learning program that creates a success blueprint by developing psychological resilience and the following character building skills:

Self-esteem—Courage and inner strength

Optimism—Possibility thinking

Wisdom—Problem-solving skills and judgment

Discipline—Persistence and motivation

Compassion—Social sensitivity and relationships

Healthy Life Choices—Nutrition, exercise, and environment

Since our children are the light of our future, how children think now will collectively determine how the world thinks and thus how we survive and thrive as a global community.

In addition to the butterfly blanket, which serves as an anchor or trigger for possibility thinking, a CD is included with guided imagery to direct optimistic and optimal thinking, problem-solving skills, and healthy life choices in children. The accompanying storybook provides engaging characters that children can identify with and relate to and then act out desirable roles through puppets and pantomimes. The puppets promote interactive, experiential learning that integrates your child's success blueprint.

Please inquire on workshops and teleseminars for parent groups, educators, and early childhood associations and organizations.

For sustained success and developmental growth, programs are also being developed for children (ages 7–12) and teens (ages 13–18).

Other Books by Edie Raether

Why Cats Don't Bark
Unleash Your PowerZone: Intuitive Intelligence—The Other IQ

By igniting your passion and purpose, you will unleash your PowerZone and master change from the "insight out". Discover your core genius and soul's code to express your authentic self and achieve optimal performance. The enlightening "aha"s will compel you to walk your talk and transform knowledge into knowing and success into significance.

Forget Selling! 12 Principles of Influence and
Persuasion in Sales, Leadership, and Life

Applying these 12 principles will make the difference between hoping for success and having it. Discover why traditional selling is no longer effective and how you can create a powerful sphere of influence that produces "yes" and predictable compliance by understanding the DNA of influence and the power of persuasion. Learn the power of leverage from left-brain logic and language to right-brain gut guidance and the silent sell.

Sex for the Soul: Seven Secrets of
Sensual Intimacy for Spiritual Ecstasy

By bringing the sacred to the sensual and the sexual to the spiritual, *Sex for the Soul* provides a prescription for bliss. By reclaiming our instinctual passions we experience the "white magic" of an empowering intimacy, fostered by love, honor, and devotion. Challenging the interpersonal exploitation of the robotic sex epidemic, the seven secrets reveal spiritual sex as a wedding of animal and angel for the ecstatic affirmation and renewal of human love.

Anthologies with Edie Raether

Rekindling the Human Spirit

Walking with the Wise

Magnetic Leadership

Fantastic Customer Service Inside and Out

How You Can Increase Your Sales in Any Economy

Life, Work & Money from a Woman's Perspective

303 Solutions for Accomplishing More in Less Time

303 Solutions for Developing the Leadership in You

303 Solutions for Dropping Stress and Finding Balance

Available at *www.raether.com*

Mastering Change—Audio and Video Programs

*Motivational and Inspirational Programs for
Personal and Professional Development*

*LeaderShift for TeamThink:
Communications and Presentation Skills*

MindShift: Sales and the Psychology of Selling

Health and Healing for Wellness and Stress Management

Parenting Effectiveness

Hypnosis for Behavioral Change: Addictions-Fears-Performance

Golf—"In the Zone": Mastering the Inner Game of Golf

Available at *www.raether.com*